JOURNEY INTO GOD

John Coblentz

Faith Builders Resource Group

JOURNEY INTO GOD

Faith Builders Resource Group, 28527 Guys Mills Rd., Guys Mills, PA 16327.

ISBN: 978-1-935972-13-6

Cover Design: Kyle Brubaker

Available from Christian Learning Resource. To order or request information, please call 1-877-222-4769 or email clr@fbep.org.

Faith Builders Resource Group is a division of Faith Builders Educational Programs. Faith Builders Resource Group is dedicated to building the Kingdom of God by partnering with conservative Anabaptist communities to identify needs and to address them with services and materials that honor Christ and strengthen His church. For more information, email fbresource@fbep.org. To learn more about Faith Builders Educational Programs, visit www.fbep.org.

Printed in the United States of America.

Contents

Foreword 5

Chapter 1. God Is 9

Chapter 2. God's Self-Disclosure 19

Chapter 3. Knowing God 39

Chapter 4. God is Holy 55

Chapter 5. God is Love 65

Chapter 6. God is Good 81

Chapter 7. God is Faithful 97

Chapter 8. God Is Righteous 115

Chapter 9. God is Sovereign 137

Chapter 10. God is Relational 159

Chapter 11. God is Omnipotent 179

Chapter 12. God is Omniscient 193

†

FOREWORD

Recently I was in a Maryland town with an old church that I had heard had connections with the Underground Railroad. Stopping by, I found that a yard sale was happening in a side room, but otherwise the church was dark. After looking at the sale items for a bit I headed through a door that led toward the darkened sanctuary. I sat in a pew, my eyes adjusting, catching a muted glimpse of the stained glass. Somewhere around here, I had been told, were tunnels and rooms used to hide slaves. I looked for more doorways and found steps leading down. A kitchen, a workshop, the dining room—but no tunnels. I was disappointed and ready to move on.

I returned to the yard sale to see if the others in our party were finished. While I waited, I asked one of the ladies handling sales if she could tell me anything about the history of the church. "Yes," she replied. "And would you like to walk around?" My quick affirmative started the adventure. The lights came on. The architecture of the church appeared. Our little group heard the story of the church. In the 1700s a fort stood on this site, commissioned by General Braddock. To increase security, trenches were dug throughout the fort. After the fort was decommissioned, a church was built over the trenches, which then formed a labyrinth of passages and rooms perfect for hiding slaves on their way north to freedom. Then the guide directed us to a door I hadn't seen. We went down into the trenches. We walked the tunnels and saw the rooms where slaves stayed for a night or two before the next leg on their freedom journey. We looked through the narrow outside entrance down to the creek where slaves hid, waiting for the signal to run up the hill and enter the safety of the church. What a delightful, meaningful tour! The guide had transformed my experience of the church.

I enjoy traveling, visiting historically significant places, tasting other foods, and getting close to different cultures. Most of my travel highlights have involved the efforts of tour guides, guides who know what they are describing and know how to capture something of the significance and wonder in what they are describing. John is that kind of guide—he lives what he writes. These are not words wrung from the hands of a paid writer but the heartbeat of a man who is on this path of knowing God.

When Jesus was asked to distill all good teaching to its essence, he quoted a passage from Deuteronomy: "The LORD our God, the LORD is One. You shall love the LORD your God with all your heart and with all your soul and with all your might" (Deuteronomy 6:4-5, ESV). Embedded in Jesus' words is the implication that you and I are fundamentally beings that love. And, as beings that love, there is no object of our love that is more true, beautiful, good, or worthy than the God of Abraham and Paul. Seek first God. Get this right and everything else becomes right. Touring a church from the Civil War era or walking the Great Wall of China—whatever the historical or cultural attraction, as fascinating as it may be, is but a light shadow of the opportunity we have to journey into God.

This journey is not merely one of a tourist: collecting sights, sounds, and smells to add to our growing collection of museum artifacts. No, it is the journey of a pilgrim, a seeker. It is the difference between merely knowing about God and knowing God. The first is necessary for the second but is no substitute for loving, obeying, and following God. Yes, if our love for God is to grow, it is vital to develop a rich and accurate way of thinking about and describing Him. *Journey into God* adds to our vocabulary about God. It helps to paint a biblically-congruent and Christ-centered picture of God. But in the midst of the description we are continually called to look beyond the words and maps to the One being described.

Journey into God is a field guide, helping us to understand what we are seeing and experiencing as we walk through life. John does not ignore the questions, the difficulties, or the confusing aspects of coming to know God; he helps us see them as opportunities to go deeper and further. *Journey into God* is an invitation to put energy and intention into responding to God's heart for relationship. It is an invitation to enter into the mystery that is God.

I offer these ideas for benefiting from this book:

- *Journey into God* has 12 chapters. This makes it convenient to spend a month in each chapter: taking time daily to read the text, work through the exercises, and meditate on related passages of Scripture (finding these passages is part of the joy).
- Use *Journey into God* in an existing small group, Sunday School class, or cell group. Dedicate one quarter or one year of your group's focus to knowing God.
- Married couples could read this book to each other. They could agree on which exercises to explore.
- Families may want to use *Journey into God* as a part of their family devotional time.
- Churches could use *Journey into God* as the basis for an ongoing series of Wednesday evening discussions.

— Steven R. Brubaker

GOD IS

But without faith it is impossible to please Him, for he who comes to God must believe that He is, and that He is a rewarder of those who diligently seek Him.

HEBREWS 11:6

The first step in any walk with God is a step of faith. Like the first step of a young child, it can be filled with wonder, fear, excitement, and the encouraging cries of delighted onlookers. God is. Whether we step from unbelief, confusion, frustration, ignorance, or bitter denial into that place of persuasion, it is a step of faith. Whether the means by which we are finally convinced to make the step include coaxing, argument, or the life of a believer, we must make the step by faith.

"He who comes to God must believe that He is," the writer to the Hebrews tells us.

God IS. Have you stumbled here? Wondered? Doubted?

Half a century ago, A. W. Tozer wrote:

> What comes into our minds when we think about God is the most important thing about us. The history of mankind will probably show that no people has ever risen above its religion, and man's spiritual history will positively demonstrate that no religion has ever been greater than its idea of God. Worship is pure or base as the worshiper entertains high or low thoughts of God.

> For this reason the gravest question before the Church is always God Himself, and the most portentous fact about any man is not what he at a given time may say or do, but what he in his deep heart conceives God to be like. We tend by a secret law of the soul to move toward our mental image of God. This is true not only of the individual Christian, but of the company of Christians that composes the Church. Always the most revealing thing about the Church is her idea of God, just as her most significant message is what she says about Him or leaves unsaid, for her silence is often more eloquent than her speech. She can never escape the self-disclosure of her witness concerning God.[1]

Over the years of my ministry, I've met many young people who have grown up in Christian homes. They've been taught about God from their mother's ankle. And as children, they believed. They loved Bible stories. God created the world. God parted the waters. God rained down food. God demolished enemy armies. God multiplied a few loaves of bread to feed thousands. God enabled people to walk out of prison, walk through fire, and walk on water. God healed the sick and raised the dead.

But eventually we need more than stories about God. We want to know Him personally. Many Christian young people remember giving their hearts to God at a tender age. It felt good. Fear and guilt were replaced with happiness and a feeling of deep inner cleansing. All was fine for a time.

These young Christians were advised to read their Bibles and pray daily if they wanted to grow and please God. Many did. But after a time the good feelings evaporated. Growing up didn't seem to help. Insecurity, disagreements with parents, pressures from peers, temptations, boyfriends, girlfriends, and acne got more attention than Bible reading. Prayer didn't help much. The God who parted the seas and raised the dead didn't seem to care about the embarrassment of a bad complexion.

Even after a few years, when they realized a new zit was not a sign of the end times and they were serious again about seeking God, they felt frustrated. The Bible was still stale reading. Prayers still didn't seem to go anywhere or do anything. God seemed "out there" somewhere in the hazy blue yonder, disconnected from real life.

"Christianity seems to work for everyone else," one young lady told me, "but not for me. I try to find Him, but He isn't there."

But it isn't just young people who struggle with knowing God "for real." Sometimes our understanding of Christian experience has been so long defined by generations of practice we assume being a Christian is doing what our fathers and mothers have done. We go to the right places and avoid the wrong places. We say the right words and don't say the bad words. We wear the right clothes. We don't steal or lie or cheat. We don't smoke or drink or look at pornography (mostly). We go to church and are taught all other denominations are worldly and unsound. We are busy enough we don't really have time to realize our lives are running on empty and our hearts are yearning for something more.

That is, until we meet individuals in whose heart a fire glows. They know God. They love Jesus with a passion. We too want that life! But we don't have a clue how to get it.

We live in a world that is not God-friendly. The world system is not tuned to Him nor interested in tuning in. The pace of life and the values consistently held before us through advertising do not move us toward God. Instead, they create fog, dull our spiritual appetites, feed other desires, and create delusions.

In *Growing Your Soul*, Neil Wiseman identifies six conditions in our times that increase our "hunger for the holy": 1) Moral erosion—a decreasing clarity about right and wrong. 2) High-tech confusion—our preoccupation with new gadgets that flash and bleep and stimulate our senses. 3) Good life seductions—the obsession to have comfort at our fingertips. 4) Ceaseless motion—always having something going, always in a rush. 5) Shallow religion—quick, tasty, and on the run. 6) An unsatisfied self—empty lives and undernourished hearts.[2] These conditions, says Wiseman, make us emptier and hungrier.

On the one hand, I agree with Wiseman. But on the other, it seems to me that the same things could be hindrances to hunger for God. It is true that these things make our hearts emptier. But it is also true that they drug the soul. They soothe the feelings and dull the mind. They keep us from asking hard questions, from doing things meaningful, and from discovering and believing in God. Although they starve the spirit (and thus increase hunger), they gratify our hunger pains with spicy living and give the illusion that this is the good life. Selfishness feels good even though it isn't good for us.

God is.

The most fundamental reality is God. Everything else derives from Him—everything came from Him and would not exist were it not for Him.

Your faith in God does not make Him real. Your unbelief in Him does not alter who He is in the least iota. The reality of God does not depend on your faith or your unbelief, your ideas or your feelings, your moods or your attitudes, your praises or your complaints. You cannot make Him more or less real or change who He is by any of your responses. God is.

You can, of course, change your perception of Him. "The fool has said in his heart, 'There is no God'" (Psalm 14:1). We can change from the folly of believing "He isn't" to the wisdom of affirming "He is." The Scriptures assert that this perception is fundamental to all knowing. "The fear of the Lord is the beginning of wisdom, and the knowledge of the Holy One is understanding" (Proverbs 9:10). When we accept the reality of God, we can begin the lifelong and soul-changing experience of not only learning to know Him, but also seeing all things in that true light.

In the process, we will form misconceptions and need to correct them with fresh discoveries, much as we do in the physical world. Discovering electricity did not automatically give us all the knowledge about electricity. Scientists discovered new characteristics of electricity as they proceeded, and thus corrected mistaken ideas and found new ways to use it.

People have always been fascinated by discoveries in the created world—not only electricity, but gravity, motion, DNA, quarks, antibiotics, species, galaxies, black holes. Yet all these things were made by Him and for Him. God upholds all things in continued existence by His command.

If everything that exists is an expression of God, then every new discovery is another glimpse into this wonderful Person who made it and sustains it. Every discovery should be another reason to assert His glory and seek His person. Surely the Creator is more worthy than His work of our consideration and discovery, of our time and energy, and of our yearning to know and experience.

Still, we may struggle. How do we *know* God is? We have the evidence in creation. We have the logical assumption that phenomenal design demands an intelligent Designer. We have the testimony of many who have "walked with Him" and "talked with Him," experiencing His miraculous work in their lives. But does this *prove* God is?

None of these things gives us absolute certainty. As the writer to early Jewish Christians said, "He who comes to God must believe that He is." The step into knowing God is a step of faith. It is saying in our hearts, "I will believe in Him."

Sometimes even Christians have not been satisfied with faith. They think that until they have proof, they will not believe. Some even claim to have proof. But if we had absolute proof, we would not need faith. We believe God is, exactly because we cannot unequivocally prove that He is. Faith is a necessity.

Our skeptical, science-cultured society often scoffs at faith. Placing one's life on the line of faith is considered foolish. But consider—is it any less risky to place one's life on the line of unbelief? Is it wiser to assume that God *isn't* and hang one's whole life and destiny on that unbelief than to assume that God *is* and hang one's whole life and destiny on that faith? We don't have absolute certainty with unbelief in God any more than we have it with faith in God. Actually, we must ignore huge amounts of evidence if we decide not to believe in God.

So we must start with faith in order to know Him.

For some people this is a difficult struggle. For others it is less so. I grew up in a Christian home, and although I sometimes wondered if God was real, my struggle was not so much whether to believe in God as it was the yearning to grow in faith. But others describe a different experience. Nicole Cliffe grew up in an atheist home and was quite happy not to believe in God. She says initially she had a rather "snarky" approach to religion, but after developing friendships with Christians, she "thought them frequently charming in their sweet delusion."

Two turning points, however, hit quite unexpectedly. The first was a difficult time with one of her children. Without thinking, one day she said to an empty room, "Be with me." Although she was not conscious of any deep yearnings, the reality was that she was up against something beyond her resources. That situation resolved, however, and she went on with life.

The second incident came as she was surfing the internet one day and came across the obituary of a Christian author. Here is her description: "A few minutes into reading the piece, I burst into tears. Later that day, I burst into tears again. And the next day. While brushing my teeth, while falling asleep, while in the shower, while feeding my kids, I would burst into tears."

What was so disconcerting to Nicole was that this behavior was so uncharacteristic of her. She had been a happy, contented person. But she began reading books by Christians, and the tears kept flowing. Finally, she emailed a Christian friend, asking if they could meet to talk about Jesus. About an hour before the appointed time of their meeting, suddenly, Nicole came to the realization that she believed in God and specifically she believed "that Jesus really was who he said he was."[3]

For everyone who comes to God, faith is a personal step. No one can believe for us. Whether we come gladly in relief or unexpectedly through pure grace or stubbornly or through the testimony of others, we must come in faith.

God is. But I must believe that He is.

Faith is a heart assurance.

We have said that God is and that we must believe that He is. What does it mean to believe in God? What is faith?

According to a variety of polls, the vast majority of Americans believes in God. The same polls show, however, that this belief is quite benign. The "faith" of many people seems to be little more than a mental assent that doesn't take God too seriously.

Biblical faith is an assurance in the deepest part of our being. "For with the heart one believes unto righteousness" (Romans 10:10). Faith is not simply knowing a fact, it is trusting a Person. It is not simply an affirmative response to another person's question, whether from a friend or a pastor, nor is it alone the repetition of an orthodox creed, much as those may be expressions of faith. Rather, faith is a settled affirmation in the heart. It is a breakthrough from trying to live by our own understanding into the commitment to live life according to the full reality of God.

The heart's assurance directs the life.

According to James, faith in God may be either dead or alive. The difference, he points out, is whether that faith finds expression in the way we live. He writes, "What does it profit, my brethren, if someone says he has faith but does not have works? Can faith save him? If a brother or sister is naked and destitute of daily food, and one of you says to them, 'Depart in peace, be warmed and filled,' but you do not give them the things which are needed for the body, what does it profit? Thus also faith by itself, if it does not have works, is dead" (James 2:14–17).

Learning to live by the reality of God is life-changing. God is not a Sunday God. That is, He is not simply someone to preach about, sing about, and study for a couple of boring hours the first day of the week—after which, we can get on with the more practical and exciting activities of life. Nor is He a devotions God. He is saddened if we spend ten minutes each morning or evening (or worse, fifteen minutes, or worse yet, an hour) pushing ourselves to read a chapter in the Bible so we can go about our day with an easy conscience, expecting Him to work things out for us because we had our devotions.

Faith enables us to walk with God—to live our lives in fellowship with Him. When we believe He is and He is God—almighty, everywhere, all the time, gloriously real—we want Him present when we work, meet people, face problems, eat, relax, face temptations, stumble, and make decisions. We want Him present when we relate to difficult people. We want Him present when we experience personal needs. We want Him to open our eyes to His intentions for us every day, so every day can be a day of worship, every activity can be enjoyed in His company, every problem can become a means of knowing Him better, and every person with whom we interact can receive something of His presence through us.

Faith in God is walking with God.

If we say we believe in God and all it means is that we pray in high tenor and listen to a sermon on Sunday, and then we forget about Him until the next scheduled recital, we are only fooling ourselves. We are certainly not fooling Him.

Dead faith is full of words and empty of life.

Living faith—faith that saves—is living in His presence. It is inviting the reality of God into all we are and say and do. It means honoring His deity—His words are God-words, and we want to hear them, understand them, and follow them. His acts are God-acts, and we want to experience them, talk about them, and remember them. His plans are God-plans, and we beg to be part of them, we pray them forward, and we immerse our hearts in them so we can cooperate with them play-by-play.

Faith rests in unseen reality.

God proper has no skin.

We have many evidences of God, and we will explore them in the next chapter. The heavens, the earth, and our own humanity declare God's existence in many ways and in powerful arguments. But God is always above and beyond hard evidence. God is Spirit.

Our faith is bolstered by evidence in the elements—the design, the complexity, the beauty, the power, the vastness, the intricacy—but that is still not God proper. Likewise, our faith gets a boost from the reasoning ability, feelings, being, persona, worship, yearnings, and morality we know and observe in ourselves and fellow human beings. Faith in God gets (or is supposed to get) the strongest supporting evidence on earth from the love Christians show to each other. (We could do with a little improvement there.) But humans are not God proper—not even redeemed humans, and not even when they love profoundly.

God is Spirit.

The bottom line is that reason—much as we use it and need it—isn't sufficient by itself to get us into God. Nor are our feelings (for which most of us are terribly grateful certain times of the day or week or month!).

We come to God by faith. When the chips are all down, we come to Him. We throw ourselves upon Him in a trusting heap of disaster and surrender. I do not mean we must cast all dignity away to believe in God. We must cast away the foolish kind—the kind that pats ourselves on the back for finally having arrived or figured something out or achieved something far beyond everyone else.

The heart that trusts Him, that says unequivocally, "He's God, and He's my God forever, come what may," is the heart that finds dignity and identity for real. We never want any other.

WALKING WITH GOD

Write a description of your own journey with God. Think about these questions. You don't need to answer all of them, but describe your journey honestly.

1. What were your God-concepts as a child?
2. When did you first experience yearning for God? Can you describe what was in your heart?
3. Who are the significant people along the way who helped or hindered you in pursuit of God?
4. What events in your life have been significant in shaping you?
5. How have books or authors helped?
6. What has been your most significant hindrance in pursuing God?
7. Have you been mostly driven by love, yearning, guilt, fear, or pressure to conform? Or have you experienced apathy instead?
8. In what ways do you find yourself drawn to God? In what ways have you struggled in accepting God or believing in God?
9. What has been the most convincing evidence to you for God's existence?

Notes

1. A. W. Tozer, *The Knowledge of the Holy* (New York: Harper & Row Publishers, 1961), 9.

2. Neil B. Wiseman, *Growing Your Soul* (Grand Rapids: Fleming H. Revell, 1996), 14-25.

3. Nicole Cliffe, "How God Messed Up My Happy Atheist Life," *Christianity Today*, May 20, 2016, http://www.christianitytoday.com/ct/2016/june/nicole-cliffe-how-god-messed-up-my-happy-atheist-life.html.

2

GOD'S SELF-DISCLOSURE

Can you search out the deep things of God?
Can you find out the limits of the Almighty?
They are higher than heaven—what can you do?
Deeper than Sheol—what can you know?
Their measure is longer than the earth
And broader than the sea.

JOB 11:7–9

No one knows who the Son is except the Father, and who the Father is except the Son, and the one to whom the Son wills to reveal Him.

LUKE 10:22

As Zophar indicated to Job in the verses above, God is beyond us. His infinity defies our comprehension. We are in kindergarten trying to understand advanced calculus. Like toddlers discussing with each other their understanding of major events in life—the birth of a sibling, their parents' marriage, the death of a grandparent—we attempt to speak of Him whom we cannot fully comprehend. And we make a good many blunders along the way.

Were it not that God has chosen to reveal Himself to us, we would be mostly in the dark. We'd be left with only the terrible misunderstandings about God spawned by fallen imaginations through the centuries. It would be each man's idea against every other man's idea, a dreary assortment of half-truths and untruths.

I will not spend time trying to prove that the God of the Bible, the God of the Judeo-Christian tradition, is the true God. That is another issue quite beyond the scope of this book, and others are far better equipped than I to do that.

I am addressing those who have accepted the reality of this God by faith, but are struggling to move forward in acquaintance with Him. And I'm grateful that God has chosen to reveal Himself. We are not left to our own devices to find Him.

Because God is God, anything we see or hear or read or feel or otherwise understand about Him is only a fraction of who He is. That's likely one of the reasons God forbids pictures or images of Himself. In their finiteness, they distort rather than reveal. It would be like holding up a blade of grass to show someone what the universe is. We would be looking at a misrepresentation, not an insight.

If we are to know God, we must pay careful attention to the ways God has chosen to reveal Himself to us. In this chapter we will look through three windows—nature, the Bible, and Jesus.

General Revelation

> The heavens declare the glory of God;
> And the firmament shows His handiwork.
> Day unto day utters speech,
> And night unto night reveals knowledge.
> There is no speech nor language
> Where their voice is not heard.
> Their line has gone out through all the earth,
> And their words to the end of the world.
> *Psalm 19:1–4*

God is the Creator. He spoke the world into existence—land and seas, plants and trees, insects, birds, and animals. He created the heavenly bodies—the moon and stars; planets, comets, and galaxies; black holes and exploding novas and supernovas.

God's creation proclaims His power and glory. The world and all that is in it, the universe and all its vastness declare, "GOD IS!" In recent decades, Christian philosophers and scientists have articulated the argument of intelligent design, saying the complexity and order of nature demand an explanation other than chance plus time, which is essentially what evolution argues. Nothing comes from nothing.

This argument is powerful enough that in 2004, Antony Flew, an eighty-one-year-old philosopher who was a voice of atheism for more than fifty years, changed his mind and announced he believed in God. Flew pointed to the "integrative complexity of creation" as one reason for his change.[1]

Even without the benefit of telescopes and microscopes, without understanding molecules or DNA or microbiology or galaxies or light-years, the Apostle Paul wrote, "For since the creation of the world God's invisible qualities—his eternal power and divine nature—have been clearly seen, being understood from what has been made" (Romans 1:20, NIV). In other words, just looking at the marvels of nature shows us that God exists and that He is powerful. The message in nature is clear enough without any manmade lenses that all people on earth are responsible to believe in God. In Paul's words, "They are without excuse" (v. 20, NKJV).

So, one of the avenues to knowing God is through His creation. God's creation tells us He is.

God's creation also tells us He is powerful. Nature pulsates with power. Niagara Falls powers generators that can produce up to 4.5 million kilowatts of power. A bolt of lightning three hundred yards long produces approximately one billion volts of electricity and superheats air to ten thousand degrees, roughly twice the temperature on the sun's surface. Even so, this is as nothing compared to the power of the sun that warms us daily from a distance of ninety-three million miles.

God's creation not only awes us, but it also delights us. Look at the majesty of mountains and glaciers, the splendor of fall colors, the dazzle of cascading waterfalls, the kaleidoscope of colors and markings on fish in a coral reef, the dizzying depth and breadth of the Grand Canyon, the towering trunks of giant sequoias, the dainty anthers and petals of flowers—all shapes and sizes and hues. Taste the spices in chili, the tang in citrus, the mouth-watering flavor of bacon, the wet sweetness of a melon, the crisp flavor of carrots, the seasoned goodness of a grilled steak or fried mushrooms or battered fish, the succulence of baked chicken, the tartness of berries, the frothy flavor of your favorite shake, the wholesome taste of corn and beans and cabbage and broccoli, the crunch of roasted and salted peanuts, almonds, cashews, pecans, and macadamias.

God could have made one kind of tree, one kind of vegetable, one kind of fruit, one kind of fish, straight riverbeds, standard shorelines, and one-size mountains. But He gave us this earth teeming with life, fantastic in variety and complexity, so every day of our lives we can be delighted by sights and smells and sounds and tastes and sensations that declare He is, so at every turn of our lives we are reminded that God made us and sustains us and is fully able to care for us.

The message of God in creation is a message we can read every day in the clouds, in the sky, in the grass, and on the wind. We can hear it in the waves and waterfalls, in the chirping and squawking and screaming and trilling of the birds, and in the chatter of the animals. We can see it in the face of the baby and the grey hair of the elderly. We can observe it in the laws by which things run—gravity and motion, time and space, aerodynamics, kinetic energy, electricity, thermodynamics—names we have given to nature's habits that are held in place by God's word. Yes, in all creation every day God is speaking, sending clear messages of His goodness, power, and glory.

Unfortunately we sometimes walk around this beauty and complexity and provision and constancy lamenting, "I can't hear God saying anything to me."

Suppose a friend sent you a dozen roses. You would look at them, exclaim over their beauty, sniff their aroma, and place them where you could be reminded of your friend's thoughtfulness and love. The roses would be a distinct and clear message from your friend's heart.

How is it we find it hard to see and feel and hear the goodness of God who "daily loads us with benefits" (Psalm 68:19)? Why shouldn't we let His flowers and His food, His gardens and His parks, His panoramic beauty in the sky and on the land, and His constant deluge of thoughtful tokens warm our hearts as kind reminders of His care and interest in us?

I like Elizabeth Browning's words:

> Earth's crammed with heaven,
> And every common bush afire with God,
> But only he who sees takes off his shoes;
> The rest sit round and pluck blackberries.

To clarify, nature is an expression of God, not God Himself, as the pantheist wrongly believes. We'd be foolish and unthoughtful to lavish more attention and praise on the roses sent by a friend than on the friend who sent them. Creation is incredibly beautiful and expressive, and we are wise to see God in the greatest as well as the tiniest specimen. But we are fools if we let worship of the Creator descend to idolatry of creation.

WALKING WITH GOD

Following are exercises for expanding your acquaintance with God through nature:

1. Take a walk. Stop everywhere you see beauty and let your heart and mind take it in. Just enjoy it. When you come back, make a list of what you remember, what hit your senses, and what lingers in your heart.
2. Find a place where all that comes to your senses is from nature—all sights, sounds, and smells. As you meditate, let your heart take in your surroundings and open your heart to God solely for experiencing Him (that is, not in order to learn something or so you can write something down).
3. You might begin a nature journal, recording glimpses of God in creation.
4. You might begin a collection of hymns, verses, and poems that speak of God in creation.

5. As you begin to see and hear God in creation, you will want to respond in prayer, praise, or thanksgiving. Writing out those expressions can be meaningful both for clarity in what your heart is experiencing as well as enabling you to remember your blessings. (Writing responses to God is analogous to sending a thank-you to the friend who sent you flowers.)
6. Many people are too busy or distracted to notice God in nature. Schedule time for listening to and looking for God's messages to you in nature either in solitude or with a friend. If necessary, take time to write out your plans to designate time for communing with God through creation.

Special Revelation

Although nature expresses God's creativity, power, and providence, much about God cannot be known through creation. God is a person, and having personality, He communicates through language and actions the thoughts and feelings and attitudes, the plans and intentions and wishes, and the qualities of being that make Him who He is. He wants to express and be understood, to love and be loved, to tell and hear, to receive others into His heart and be received in the hearts of others. God is a person.

So God speaks.

And God hears.

"God . . . at various times and in various ways spoke in time past to the fathers by the prophets" (Hebrews 1:1). Sometimes God spoke through angels, His special messengers. Sometimes He moved in the hearts of people without audible sound, but with unmistakable clarity. At other times He spoke into the ears of people, audibly breaking into their awareness. Some of these messages were personal, addressed primarily to the hearer. Sometimes the messages were given to a person to share with a larger group—most often the person's own ethnic people, but occasionally to a neighboring group.

Many of these messages and histories of God's working, speaking, and interacting with people were written down. They were seen as divine interventions and interactions—special revelations to be heard and told and recorded. Jesus, along with the Jewish people, referred to the written record of God's works and words in the Old Testament as "the Scriptures" (literally, writings) or "the Law and the Prophets," or sometimes to the legal portion as "the Law." Today we refer to the whole collection of writings, including the New Testament, as the Bible, God's Word, or the Scriptures.

The largest portions of the Bible are histories—stories of God's people as individuals, families, and communities. The Old Testament books from Genesis to Esther are mostly history. In the New Testament, the Gospels and Acts form the story section.

These stories record how ordinary people interacted with God. Either they believed God and experienced His work on their behalf or they did not believe God and suffered for their unbelief. Or perhaps more realistically, they portray a kind of "in between," an imperfect faith that grew.

From these stories we learn that the greatest and wisest and most influential men and women were not great in themselves. They did not attain greatness through the common means by which people pursue greatness—wealth, might, position, and so on. They had faults and problems, but they knew God, believed in Him, and tried to live accordingly (however imperfectly on all three counts).

Another significant section of the Bible is the collection of messages God gave to His people through prophets, people God gifted with the ability to hear from Him and speak as His representatives. God often gave prophets power to do miracles—heal the sick, control weather, find lost items, bless or curse lives or possessions, send fire, and confuse or conquer enemies. These miracles were often seen as confirming the validity of the message from God.

The true prophet seldom won popularity contests. His message was often one of rebuke or correction to people who wanted to live by their own standards and resented being reminded of God and His ways. Most of the prophets were slapped around or thrown out at some point in their ministry. Many prophets wrote down their messages from God. These writings, too, were preserved and collected as special revelations from God.

The prophetic section of the Old Testament stretches from Isaiah through Malachi, and the corresponding section in the New Testament includes the writings of Paul, James, Peter, and John.

In addition to the stories and the prophecies were literary pieces—songs, proverbs, allegories, and musings of the wise. These writings are often referred to as "wisdom literature." They express worship and pour out praise or petition or lamentation or perplexity to God for who He is and what He has done. They capture profound truth in a saying, in a symbol or series of symbols, or in a song or story in memorable style. The literary structure, choice of words, symbolism, and subtle play on words and meanings combine to form beauty and unleash the power of heartfelt human expression. The books of Job through Song of Solomon, as well as Lamentations, comprise the artistic literature of the Bible, although many of the writings of the prophets in both the Old and New Testaments are done in poetic style as well.

All this is collected in the Bible. The collection itself is amazing, encompassing more than forty writers, scattered over fifteen hundred years, written in several languages, coming from a variety of cultures, expressed in the full range of literary genres, and best of all, showing us a God we can count on.

The special revelation of God is a wealth of guidance, encouragement, promise, wisdom, worship, and blessing. We are told to read the Bible. We hear testimonies of people who have been blessed and guided and saved through reading the Bible. We have God's Word readily available in a variety of translations and paraphrases. We have Bible commentaries, Bible encyclopedias, Bible dictionaries, study Bibles, and Bible atlases to help us understand every book, writer, setting, chapter, verse, phrase, and word.

But amidst all this Bibliorama, sometimes we find our own hearts embarrassingly unresponsive. We read the Bible and we are bored. Our minds wander. We'd like to give a testimony, too, but who wants to hear that we fell asleep before the end of the third verse?

Don't despair. Just as we can miss God's voice in nature, we can also miss God in His Word. This might be because we are looking for the wrong thing or approaching the Bible in the wrong way. More often we are simply caught between the world of the senses and the realm of the spirit without bridge-building experience. The pace of our culture and increasing addiction to bite-sized glitz do not help us.

We live in an age of consumerism. We want. We shop. We buy. We use. We expect results—now! If it doesn't work, we want our money back. If it doesn't last, we throw it away. If it costs too much, we complain. If we aren't satisfied, we call customer service. After all, the advertisement said satisfaction is guaranteed.

God is not a product.

The Bible is not about getting what we want. God's Word is an expression of Himself, inviting us to learn to know Him. *This is the most fundamental reality of special revelation.* It is the most important thing to know about the Bible. It is God's revelation of Himself. We should read the Bible to learn to know Him, not to get something, not to feel better, not to do an assignment, not even to "have devotions." The hymn writer Mary Lathbury said it so well: "Beyond the sacred page I seek Thee, Lord; My spirit pants for Thee, O living Word!"

God's Word shows us who He is.

In God's Word we constantly find either direct descriptions of God or brilliant reflections. Through direct statements or living stories, we learn over and over that God is holy, loving, righteous, merciful, all-sufficient, eternal, and omnipotent. We observe God's nature—His heart and disposition. We learn about His purposes and His methods. We discover what He likes and what He doesn't like. We see how He responds to people and situations.

God's Word shows us what God does.

God does things only God can do. He is not limited by time and space. He does not grow tired or lose interest. He is not stumped by problems. In fact, the worse the difficulty, the greater the opportunity for God to do a God-thing—a miracle.

Someone has said, "When God wants to do a great work, He chooses a great difficulty. When God wants to do a really great work, He chooses an impossibility." As the angel told Mary, "With God nothing will be impossible" (Luke 1:37).

God can make a world out of nothing. He can cause water to stand up in a heap. He can make a donkey talk. He can heal sickness. He can send a swarm of hornets to chase off an army. He can cause the sun to stand still. In short, when something needs to happen, God can do it. Anything.

God's works recorded in the Bible are revelatory—they enable us to know God. They are typically recorded in story form, but sometimes they are preserved in a song or used as an illustration in a teaching section. When we read these stories with eyes of faith, our hearts are warmed, arrested, corrected, stretched, instructed, and encouraged. Sometimes we laugh—a donkey talking! And Balaam talks back to him! Sometimes we see ourselves—Sarah, eighty-nine years old, laughed when she overheard God telling her husband she would bear a son within a year. Sometimes we cringe because we don't understand—Job losing almost everything with God's permission or God destroying entire cities.

These stories affect our hearts when we read them with our eyes on God. Paul wrote, "For whatever things were written before were written for our learning, that we through the patience and comfort of the Scriptures might have hope" (Romans 15:4). Our job is not to try to figure out how God did these things—did He use lightning to light Elijah's altar, or just *bam!* shoot fire from a heavenly portal? (In any case, His aim was dead on.)

Much less are we called to judge God's actions. We are no more equipped to judge God's works than a child is able to evaluate the work of a chemical engineer. Although God does not scold us for honest questions or exploration, He calls us to trust when we do not understand.

When God does great works, He urges us to remember what He has done. Sometimes He asks His people to start a tradition to help them remember what He has done—such as the Passover meal in the Old Covenant or the Lord's Supper in the New Covenant. The psalmist helps us understand the importance of the works of God:

> The works of the Lord are great,
> Studied by all who have pleasure in them.

His work is honorable and glorious,
 And His righteousness endures forever.
He has made His wonderful works to be remembered;
 The LORD is gracious and full of compassion.
 Psalm 111:2–4

God's Word shows us God's intentions.

If we stand back and look at the messages, the stories, the commands, the promises, the songs, and the prophecies, we see a huge picture unfolding. God is not only showing us Himself, but He is also letting us know His intentions for us, for the world, for time, and for eternity. He made us. He made the world. In spite of our waywardness and sin, He is committed to carrying out His purposes.

God's intentions are bigger than "me" and broader than "now." His purposes span time, encompass all eras, and cross all cultures. We learn to know these purposes of God through *His* story in the Bible. When we begin to see God's purposes, we gain a healthy sense of humility. We have been invited to participate in something really, really big, a stupendous work of God that dwarfs everything we have seen or can imagine. The story includes us, but it is not primarily about us. The real events of history are not about kingdoms and nations and bloody heroes and emperors and conquest. The real story is what God has planned and done, what He is doing, and what He will consummate in the full revelation of His Son Jesus.

This is what the Bible is about. This is what it shows us. When we begin to glimpse—and believe—God's purposes in Jesus, we come alive with awe and gratitude. We are invited into His plan. We are personally known, loved, and welcomed into this grand scheme of God. The overarching theme of the Bible is the glory of God in Christ.

The created world gives us a great visual to understand this. Our world is a dot in the solar system. More than one million earths could fit into the sun, ninety-three million miles away. To try to put this into perspective, if our earth were a one-inch ball, the sun would be a nine-foot sphere three hundred yards away.

On our annual trip around the sun, we shuffle along at about sixty-five thousand miles per hour. Our solar system is a small speck in our Milky Way galaxy, which has an estimated two hundred billion additional stars. We are about twenty-five thousand light-years from the center of our galaxy, hustling around the center at 132 miles per second, but it still will take us 225 million years to make one revolution.

That's us in our galaxy. Astronomers estimate there are enough galaxies in the universe for every person to have several of his own. The earth is a rather small part of the universe, isn't it? And there are some seven billion individuals running around on this speck of dirt in our solar system—a barely visible dot in the Milky Way.

Isn't it humbling to think of individual persons in that vastness? These heavens "declare the glory of God"! The plan of God in Jesus is likewise astounding and humbling. To explore that, perhaps we need to move to the third "window" of God's revelation after a few reflections.

WALKING WITH GOD

Following are ways you can explore God's written revelation of Himself. Don't look at these as assignments, but as avenues to acquaintance with this wonderful Person.

1. To think about the Scriptures in a fresh way, you might spend some time observing how Jesus used the Scriptures and how He talked about them. Try scanning through a Gospel, pausing where He quoted from or spoke about the Scriptures. Or you could read and meditate on the following examples: a) Matthew 22:23–46; b) Matthew 26:53–56; c) Luke 24:25–49; d) John 5:36–47.
2. As you study, consider what Jesus had to say about the following: a) The reliability of the Scriptures; b) The intent of the Scriptures; c) The focus of the Scriptures; d) Misuse or misunderstanding of the Scriptures.
3. Evaluate your own interaction with the Scriptures. Try to describe what they mean to you in several words or phrases. What would you like to change about your interaction with the Scriptures?

4. Try writing a one or two-page summary of the story of God's work as revealed in the Bible.
5. List some of the blessings you have received through the Scriptures—favorite passages, favorite characters, or meaningful stories. Or you might recall specific ways God has spoken to you through particular verses or passages—giving comfort, encouragement, correction, or insight. How could you share these stories with fellow believers?

One verse that stood out to me was 1 John 4:4 Greater is he that is in you, then he that is in the world. the devil may have power, but his strength is limited whereas God's grace has no limit.

Personal Revelation

Creation is a window into God that reveals His power and greatness. The Bible offers a clearer revelation through which we hear God's voice, learn to know what He has done in history, and catch glimpses into His gigantic and glorious intentions, as well as His will for our lives personally. But that is not enough. Wonderful as the writings are, they fall short of showing us all about God.

God came among us in the man Jesus. Birthed of a woman, born into a Jewish family in fulfillment of many prophecies in God's written revelation, Jesus lived among us to show us the Father. In Jesus we learn God's gracious, compassionate intentions toward us. We learn that God is moved by the sin and suffering in our world, that He seeks to redeem sinners, that He invites the unworthy into His family and extends His love to those who have turned from Him, ignored Him, and even mistreated Him.

In Jesus the Father calls us to Himself. Jesus is the great message (Word) from God and the great invitation (Way) to God. We call His coming the Incarnation—God's intrusion into flesh. It is a mystery, something we could not have known or figured out on our own, and also something that extends beyond our ability to reason or explain. We are called to believe and enjoy the mystery of God among us and to experience Him by faith.

When Jesus takes up residence in us in spiritual union, we learn to know the Father personally. We are taught by the Spirit of Jesus to address Him as Papa, *Abba*, our Father. We learn that He knows us personally and thoroughly. In Jesus' terms, He knows us down to the number of "the hairs of your head" (Matthew 10:30, ESV).

Jesus taught us that He and His Father are one. "He who has seen Me has seen the Father," He said to Philip (John 14:9). What is God like? He is like Jesus—full of grace and truth, seeking the lost, committed to those who believe in Him, straightforward with the proud, rebuking the hypocritical, tender toward the downtrodden, patient with learners, protective of children, angered by oppression and greed, exuberant when sinners repent, truthful, clearly warning about the destruction of the wicked, and saddened by the selfishness, stubbornness, and hardness of the human heart. This is Jesus, and this is the heart of His Father.

The writer to the Hebrews says Jesus is the "express image" of the Father, the exact representation—a Greek term borrowed from the die imprint trade (Hebrews 1:3).

The confusing part of this reality is the humanity of Jesus. He appeared in flesh and blood. He says clearly that the Father is Spirit. So Jesus did not mean that His earthly body was a revelation of God. In His body, it seems that Jesus was intentionally nondescript. "He had no form or majesty that we should look at him, and no beauty that we should desire him," the prophet Isaiah said (Isaiah 53:2, ESV). Nearing the end of His earthly time, Jesus prayed for the restoration of His glory. "And now, O Father, glorify Me together with Yourself, with the glory which I had with You before the world was" (John 17:5).

The Incarnation, although intended to reveal the Father, was also a veiling of God. It was both a showing and a covering. The apostles understood this and spoke of Jesus' body as a veil or curtain (see, for example, Hebrews 10:20). Some who saw Him in His body actually seemed to stumble on this very point. *How can He be God? We've seen Him grow up in our town, He has brothers and sisters, He does carpentry, He eats and sleeps*. And when they nailed Him to the cross, they were fully convinced He was no more than human, for they saw Him bleed and die. "Let Him now come down from the cross," they taunted, "and we will believe Him. He trusted in God; let Him deliver Him now if He will have Him; for He said, 'I am the Son of God'" (Matthew 27:42, 43).

As a personal revelation of God, Jesus is the fulfillment of the written revelation. The prophets foretold many details of Jesus' birth, life, ministry, death, and resurrection. The Law had intricate pictures of Jesus woven into the ceremonies and rituals of the Old Covenant. Numerous characters and events in the Old Covenant were shadows, types, and signs pointing to Jesus the Messiah. Moses the prophet, Aaron the priest, David the king, the sacrificial lambs, the Passover, the Day of Atonement, the Sabbath, the Year of Jubilee, raising the brass snake on a pole, striking the rock to produce a life-giving stream of water, Abraham offering his miracle son—these people, activities, and events are rich with messages of Jesus.

Only God could plan and pull off the grand scheme of ceremonies, events, feasts, and prophecies spanning many centuries and converging in one person. We do not profess to know all that God was doing in Jesus. Nor are we called to explain everything. We are called to believe and by faith to enter into relationship with Him.

Although the work of God tells a grand story, our faith is not simply in the story. Our faith is in God. Whether we believe or disbelieve the factual details, we can still miss Him. God's great works are intended to bring us to Him.

The Jews of Jesus' day believed in God. They believed He had done miracles. They believed the factual data. They did what they understood God to be telling them to do—observe the Sabbath, keep the feasts, sing the psalms, and offer the sacrifices. But most of them missed seeing Jesus as God's Son.

If our understanding of biblical history does not lead us to Jesus, we are no better than those who study nature and deny the Creator. We have missed the very one whom both nature and the writings are intended to reveal.

Jesus taught with authority. He did not teach as other teachers who sought to understand and live out what God said in times past. Rather, He taught as the author of truth. Other teachers attempted to explain what God had done and said. Jesus spoke the will and mind of God for us. He showed us God's heart.

Jesus taught us to . . .

- Love, worship, and trust the Father.

- Dedicate ourselves to seek His kingdom, bringing about His purposes on earth.
- Live out kindness, justice, mercy, and righteousness in relating to others.
- Use our abilities and resources for the glory of God and the good of others.
- Extend love and goodwill toward those who mistreat us.
- Forgive those who hurt us and trust the Father to settle all accounts.
- Be generous to the needy, patient with the weak, and compassionate to the suffering.
- Live in spiritual union with Him.
- Expect adversity and endure it patiently.
- Believe all that is written in the Scriptures.
- Speak the truth.
- Pray trustingly to the Father in His name.

Jesus taught us not to . . .

- Worry.
- Doubt.
- Accumulate riches to ourselves.
- Seek our own glory.
- Demand our rights or seek retribution for wrongs.
- Harbor ill will or hold grudges.
- Use forceful means to protect our rights.
- Curry favor with the rich or powerful.
- Do good in order to be recognized and praised by people.
- Turn back.

Jesus did not teach these things as laws, as a second set of requirements to do or an improved version of the old Law. Rather He taught us to come into fellowship with Him and experience His life in us, and He said this way of living would then spring out of our loving, deepening relationship with Him. This is love. To live in Him is to live in love. To live in Him is to enter into fellowship with the Father, to become servant-minded toward our fellow man, and to live for the glory of God and the good of others.

What Jesus taught then, He teaches today. His message to His disciples is His message to us. When we live in union with Him, He speaks the same words to our hearts with the same authority. He is the Son of God, continually speaking the mind of God to the heart of man.

Jesus is real.

The Son of God is alive. He remains the same Jesus He was and is and will be. His life and teaching as preserved in the written records prepare us to receive Him in living reality.

God's purpose is not simply for us to believe the stories are true, or to assent to statements of truth, or just to do certain things He asks us to do. *All these things are right*. But they are not primary. Their intent is to lead us into relationship with the Father-Son-Spirit oneness where we know Him as God, believe in Him as God, worship Him as God, and love Him as God with all our heart, soul, mind, and strength.

Like the Father, the Son stretches beyond us in divine personhood. We are introduced to Him as a baby in Bethlehem who grew up to be a carpenter from Nazareth. Learning to know Him is to come into a relationship like we have never had, a relationship that offers an ocean of exploration, a new world of surprises that sometimes drops our jaws, sometimes thrills us speechless, and sometimes throws us to our knees.

It was no different for those who knew Him in the limitations of body and time. Those who encountered Him were sometimes filled with awe or terror or profound joy or all three. At times they tried to put into words who this Jesus was, and other times they told no one until years later. Descriptive words seemed either inadequate or sacrilegious. Here is a sampling of things they gasped in those exploding moments of insight:

"Behold! The Lamb of God who takes away the sin of the world!"

"You're a prophet!"

"Come see a man who told me everything I ever did!"

"You are the Messiah, the Son of the living God!"

"Truly this is the Son of God!"

"My Lord and my God!"

One of Jesus' disciples devoted a whole book to what he saw in revelation after revelation of Jesus Christ. It is filled with exclamations, graphic imagery, and scenes that nearly blind us. In this book Jesus is called the Alpha and the Omega, the First and the Last, the Beginning and the End, the Living One, the One who holds the seven stars in His right hand and walks among the seven golden lampstands, the Son of God whose eyes are like blazing fire and whose feet are like burnished bronze, the One who is holy and true, who holds the key of David, the Amen, the Faithful and True Witness, the Ruler of God's creation, the Lion of the tribe of Judah, the Root of David, the Lamb who was slain, the Holy One, Faithful and True, the Word of God, King of kings and Lord of lords, the Root and the Offspring of David, and the blazing Morning Star.

This Jesus is unparalleled. In all of human history, no person has inspired more literature, art, and music. Still, words fail us. Jesus cannot be described in full. He is to be experienced.

Jesus is the One who shows us the Father, introduces Him, and invites us into relationship with Him. Jesus the Son shares with us His own relationship with the Father, calling us sons and daughters of God, assuring us that His Father seeks to be our Father, urging us to explore that familial kinship with Him, and promising that the Father will bring it to glorious fullness in eternity.

Unfortunately, we commonly live far below our provisions. We doubt God's love for us, hold His good intentions suspect, assume we know better than He the best way to fill the emptiness in our hearts, try to make life work on our own, expend huge amounts of energy trying to solve our problems, waste a good bit more energy worrying about problems we fear we can't prevent, and go through far too much of our lives distracted, distraught, and too busy for divine fellowship.

Jesus invites us to come to Him. It is an invitation we cannot afford to ignore.

"And we know that the Son of God has come and has given us an understanding, that we may know Him who is true; and we are in Him who is true, in His Son Jesus Christ. This is the true God and eternal life"! (1 John 5:20).

WALKING WITH GOD

Following are ways for you to seek to know Jesus better:

1. Describe Him. As clearly as you can, write out what you understand about Jesus.
2. Scan one of the Gospels, pausing at the stories that arrest your attention. Imagine yourself as an onlooker. What would you want to say to Jesus in that setting? Go ahead and talk to Him. And listen.
3. Ask your acquaintances who know Jesus to tell you what He means to them or how they have learned to know Jesus. Pay attention to what they say—one way Jesus makes Himself known is through His people. You might also ask children to tell you who Jesus is.
4. Alone with Jesus, sing "Jesus, Lover of My Soul." Or sing other songs that address Him, such as "Jesus, Thou Joy of Loving Hearts," "Fairest Lord Jesus," "Jesus, the Very Thought of Thee," or "Jesus, Thy Boundless Love to Me."
5. Read about the life of Jesus. Especially if you are well-acquainted with the stories of Jesus in the Gospels, try reading a book written about Jesus. Examples:

   The Life and Teaching of Jesus Christ, by James Stewart
   The Day Christ Died, by Jim Bishop
   The Master: A Life of Christ, by John Pollock

Notes

1. James A. Beverley, "Thinking Straighter," Christianity Today, April 8, 2005, http://www.christianitytoday.com/ct/2005/april/29.80.html.

KNOWING GOD

And this is eternal life,

that they may know You,

the only true God,

and Jesus Christ,

whom You have sent.

JOHN 17:3

God is.

We believe that He is.

So where do we go from here?

This is the rub for many people. Faith does more than merely grasp the bare fact that God exists, it urges people to diligently seek Him, to set out on a journey of knowing. We are in for a lifelong progression of acquaintance that will include rough roads and pleasant wayside rests, dangerous mountain climbing and exciting explorations, up and down, over sea and under stone, but always pressing forward into knowing Him.

We believe God is personal. He is transcendent, of course, so we do not profess to understand everything about Him, but we believe He knows and feels and plans and perceives and decides and yearns and relates. He is a person in the fullest sense of personhood. We are made in His image. Whatever capacities we have in our finite condition, He has in infinity. We know—He is omniscient.

We decide—He is sovereign. We make—He creates. We exist in time and space—God is present everywhere. We measure ourselves by what we can do—for God, anything is possible.

This God has made Himself known to us. I hear Christians young and old saying they want to know God and know Him better. This has been the number one cry of my own heart for many years running. But it is not always easy to know from day to day, or even from year to year, what progress we are making.

I have been married to Barbara for more than forty years. Learning to know her has been delightful, rewarding, and life-shaping. I learned to know her by living with her—talking, planning, walking, working, playing, laughing, crying, loving, and suffering . . . together. We've faced ecstasy together. We've faced heartache together. We've shared our lives. We've stuck together through everything—the good and the bad—because we pledged to do so, and we have kept our marriage vows.

I know Barbara. I don't know everything about her, but I know her.

If we are going to learn to know God, we must live together. As I said before, it does not come about simply by "having devotions" for a certain number of minutes each day but by being devoted all the time, by sharing everything and sticking together through anything.

Knowing God is not exactly like knowing a spouse. God isn't visible. God doesn't speak audibly. God doesn't touch us and hold us close. We can't even hang up God's picture beside those of our other loved ones. God is not flesh and blood. God is Spirit. God is God.

But still God is. Oh yes, He is!

Knowing Him

We have God's glory revealed in nature, God's ways and works revealed in the Scriptures, and God's nature and person revealed in Jesus. God has indeed gone to great lengths to reveal Himself. How shall we think about knowing Him? We do well to keep a number of things clearly in mind.

Knowing God has its foundation in being known by Him.
The psalmist notes that God is intensely interested in those who seek Him, and He is disappointed that as humans we seek our own interests and walk in our own paths.

> The Lord looks down from heaven upon the children of men,
> To see if there are any who understand, who seek God.
> They have all turned aside,
> They have together become corrupt;
> There is none who does good,
> No, not one.
> *Psalm 14:2, 3*

According to Jesus, the Father is seeking true worshipers, and a primary reason for Jesus coming into the world was "to seek and to save that which was lost" (Luke 19:10). The grim reality is that we've not been merely indifferent toward God but downright obstinate in turning from God and toward our own ways.

By God's grace, many experience the yearning to know Him. As Jesus pointed out, "No one can come to Me unless the Father who sent Me draws him" (John 6:44). How we should rejoice in God's grace whenever we sense that yearning to seek God, to find Him, to know Him! "For it is God who works in you both to will and to do for His good pleasure" (Philippians 2:13).

Then why is the search for God so difficult at times? Or as one writer asks, "Why isn't God more obvious?" Why must we deal with the "hiddenness" of God? She goes on to explain, "Indeed, the belief in a God who can be easily found, and who has acted in time and space makes the hiddenness of God all the more poignant and perplexing. Theologians have offered many explanations for God's hiddenness: because God seeks to grow our faith, because our sins and disobedience hide us from God and keep us from seeing God properly, or because God loves us and knows *how much* and *how often* we need to 'find' God."[1]

We may be assured that God is not simply being difficult. Remember the lengths to which He has gone to make Himself known. Rather, our fallen condition, not only individually but also collectively, is oriented contrary to Him rather than toward Him. Knowing Him calls for a reorientation, a process that can be confusing, disappointing, and fraught with setbacks.

The writer of Hebrews hints at this when he assures us that God "is a rewarder of those who diligently seek Him" (Hebrews 11:6). Whatever confusion or sorrow attends the search, we will find Him, and the finding will more than compensate us for our pains.

Furthermore, feeling that God is hidden is partly the curse of our condition and our perspective in that condition. After we find Him, we come to understand He was coming to us long before we were coming to Him. As an anonymous hymn writer said many years ago:

> I sought the Lord, and afterward I knew
> He moved my soul to seek Him, seeking me;
> It was not I that found, O Savior true,
> No, I was found of Thee.
>
> Thou didst reach forth Thy hand and mine enfold,
> I walked and sank not on the storm-vexed sea;
> 'Twas not so much that I on Thee took hold
> As Thou, dear Lord, on me.
>
> I find, I walk, I love, but O the whole
> Of love is but my answer, Lord, to Thee!
> For Thou wert long beforehand with my soul:
> Always Thou lovedst me.

How easily we assume the wrong perspective! We think we are seeking Him, choosing Him, learning to know Him. In finding Him, we learn that He was seeking us, has chosen us, and has known us long before we sought Him.

That God has known us—not in a shallow, distant-acquaintance sort of way, but intimately cared for and loved us while we were ignorant of and indifferent toward Him—can be disconcerting. The truth of being known so thoroughly can give us the uneasy realization that we have been on candid camera even in our most secret moments.

All our words, including unspoken ones, have been clearly audible to God's ears. All our phone conversations have been tapped, and our computer usage preserved in Heaven's history.

But God is not an investigator. He runs no divine tabloid intent on collecting and publishing human garbage. He has no paparazzi among His angels.

Being known by God means being known by one whose essence is love. When our desperate seeking turns to finding, we are comforted by being known by Him. His knowing us is our salvation. Yes, He knows our sin and our weakness and our worst moments, but even knowing us at our worst, He has acted in our best interest.

Learning that God, according to His gracious heart, has been seeking us and has been acquainted with us in love is one of the delights of knowing God. It is somewhat like a young man who has guarded his love for a young woman, wishing for a relationship with her, but fearful that she isn't interested. Gathering his courage, when he finally makes his request, he discovers she has loved him for years and longed to have him ask for a relationship. Well, kind of like that, only God "knowing" us is better. It flips more breakers in our systems than any other relationship. Romance is great. It does crazy things to our hearts. But divine love beats human romance all hollow. It sets our hearts right.

Writing to the Galatian believers, Paul alludes to their former state of not knowing God. Then he says, "But now after you have known God, or rather are known by God . . . " (Galatians 4:9). In that phrase he seems to catch himself and expand his perspective. We think of our relationship from our perspective—the time we came to know Him. The true perspective and the more important one is that knowing started with God. Not only did our knowing start with God, but our relationship is sustained more by God knowing us than by us knowing Him.

This doesn't mean we leave it all up to Him. God loves the heart that seeks Him, the heart that is desperate for Him, the heart that can't get through the day without some time alone with Him, the heart that lives in continual ache for more. If it were all up to us, if it were even mostly up to our knowing Him, our relationship would be sunk.

We've got a God who knows us beyond the most loving, caring, passionate, committed heart we can imagine. And that fact keeps us seeking Him!

Knowing God is living in life.

In one of the last recorded prayers of Jesus, and arguably the most profound, Jesus indicates that a central purpose of His incarnation was to make the Father known to those who believed in Him. "I have revealed you to those whom you gave me out of the world" (John 17:6, NIV). Over and over in His earthly ministry, we see Jesus doing this.

"Your heavenly Father shows mercy and kindness to all people, giving sunshine and rain to the righteous and the unrighteous, to the deserving and the undeserving."

"He knows the number of hairs on your head and even keeps track of the ones you lose."

"He looks after sparrows and flowers."

"He has a special smile of approval for the good things you do that others don't notice."

"In Heaven, He shouts out, 'That's my girl!' or 'That's my son!' when He sees you acting as an agent of peace in this troubled world."

"He is delightedly planning awards ceremonies for those who stand up for Him, own Him, and live out His intentions in hostile settings."

"He loves when people get real with Him about their neediness. Those people capture His heart and attention."

"He despises having people pretend they have life all together, especially when they act that way as representatives of Him."

"He grieves over anyone who is spiritually lost."

"He delights in children, especially their unsophisticated faith."

"Mercy and true righteousness are huge issues with Him."

"So are injustice and hypocrisy. He is merciless with hypocrites."

"The number one thing He wants from humans is that they love Him—that they set their hearts on Him above all else."

"His heart is warmed when He sees humans loving each other in practical ways—feeding the hungry, clothing the naked, caring for the destitute, visiting those in prison—and He is moved to tears when that kind of work is done sacrificially."

"He loves to answer the prayers of those who are about His business on the earth—He'll do impossible things to demonstrate His support of them."

In my own words, this is a smattering of Jesus' teaching about His Father. Jesus didn't just stand around telling us these things, He lived this way. We could take any of these teachings and find incidents in His ministry where He showed us what it looks like. These are windows into God's heart. They show us who God is, what He likes and doesn't like, what matters to Him, and what His intentions are.

Knowing God is coming into a way of life that is filled with the presence of this God. This is eternal life. True life is knowing Him in the sense of being lovingly acquainted with Him and uniting with who He is. He quickens our hearts. We come alive to understandings, perspectives, feelings, and aspirations that are impossible to experience otherwise.

As we share in God's heart, the sobs of the downtrodden break our hearts, the cries of the lost get our attention, the needs of the world arrest and employ our resources, the tears of the penitent fill our hearts with incredible joy, our own needs wring anguished confessions at times too deep for human language. Worship courses through us, sometimes like a gentle shower, sometimes like a hurricane. We are alive with the life of Heaven.

It can be almost more than a body of flesh and bones can endure.

We see Jesus living this kind of life. Sometimes He wept, sometimes He burst out with an exclamation that made sense only to what He alone was seeing and hearing, sometimes He needed to get away to spend uninterrupted time with the Father. It is life eternal to know Him! It is the life He prayed we would experience.

Knowing God is a journey.

In this chapter I'm getting at the heart of my purpose for this book, but I need to clarify that I'm not trying to write a how-to book. I'm trying very hard not to write such a book. There is no twelve-step plan to wean us from our addictions to other gods and set us forever on the right road.

Nor are there four simple steps to peace and then we're done. Sprinkling sawdust on the trail won't help. Pouring water on your head won't automatically open the portals, nor being dipped under the water forward or backward, nor arguing about how to get the water on people properly or people into the water properly. With all respect.

This is about pointing in the right direction. This is about getting glimpses through the trees that make us break into a run. This is about passion that yearns, eyes that long for, hearts that pound. This is about parched lips. This is about chasing God.

So back to God.

God is God. If we come to Him looking for a problem-solver or a miracle-worker or a rich donor or a healer or a shame-remover or a pardoner, we've come to the right person. He's all of that and more, and most of us come through one of those doorways.

But there is a danger in coming to Him for particular needs. We can come to Him only for whatever we want Him to offer us—hopefully without too much pain. When He's done what we want, we've gotten a bargain and that's that. We're even willing to give our testimony if called upon.

God is God. Coming to Him is venturing into an ocean we cannot fathom. Staying on the beach may be pleasant enough, but it's not exploring the deep. And like most beachgoers, we may be there largely for self-interests. The soul that comes to God in shame or brokenness or sickness or trouble must eventually learn that life—true life—is not about us but about Him. He forgives our sins, heals our diseases, and rescues us from trouble not simply to make us feel better, but to deliver us from ourselves and invite us into the ocean of life.

God is God. Learning to know Him is a journey. We know that life in God is entered through His Son Jesus. Yet I'm amazed and blessed to see the entrance experiences people have in coming to God and the diversity of their continued journey into God.

Some enter through the doorway of intellectual struggle. Some arrive as emotional wrecks. Some come after a financial disaster, others through the piercing sorrow of broken relationships. Some are won by kindness. Some seemingly stumble into the kingdom almost by accident, at least, they were not planning to get there. Some come kicking, some come weeping, some try God as an experiment. Some come intending to prove God isn't, break their hard hearts on the truth of the I AM, and stay on in adoration.

About the time we think we have it nailed down to the four things a person must do to be saved, someone flies in over our heads without properly observing step three.

How hard we have tried to define salvation and quantify it so we can know if we've got it! But salvation is not so much an event to experience at a certain point in time or a possession to have or lose (lots to argue about there) as it is a Person and a relationship with that Person. When we live in Him, we live in His salvation. We need to keep the focus where it belongs—on the Savior more than on a salvation experience. "He who has the Son has life; he who does not have the Son of God does not have life" (1 John 5:12).

When we come to God, no matter what our experience, we've got a journey ahead of us. If we're basking in the sun on the beach, God will arrange the circumstances of life to urge us toward deeper waters. He wants to draw us into Himself, and He is amazingly adept at doing it.

As I indicated earlier, the "entrance experience" into the life of God varies considerably, as do the experiences along the way. I don't mean that we should seek bizarre experiences or presume that strange experiences are more authentic. I simply want to caution against trying to prescribe the experience too precisely, or worse, trying to judge the experiences of others. If we truly know God, and have restricted entrance only to those with our particular security code, it is more likely God has made Himself known to us in spite of our entrance requirements than because of them.

We are called to repentance, we are called to believe in Jesus, and we are called to be baptized. Actual experience may happen like a lightning bolt or be stretched over years. We may get things out of order, being baptized in ignorance and understanding it years later. Our initial repentance may be focused on surface behaviors, and only later do we learn the shame of the selfishness or self-righteousness in our hearts.

The more important reality is that we are truly learning to know God. When we come into the life of Jesus, we will be changed.

Having urged us away from a focus on seeking certain experiences in favor of a focus on seeking God, I want to affirm that we can expect a number of things on this journey into God. When we look at the people in the Bible who sought and found God, when we interact with people today who know Him, we find common themes.

They are alive. People who know God are opened to a world they did not experience before, and it changes the way they experience this world. They see people as souls, as humans with hopes and hungers, purpose and value, adrift or anchored, lost or found, wounded or healed, broken but redeemable. They ponder events in the light of God's reign, God's purposes, God's love, and God's presence. They value people, possessions, activities, and ideas according to the reign of God. Even as they seek Him, their life priority is to advance His kingdom. They are alive to a whole new way of loving, thinking, choosing, and living.

They are changed. People who know God cannot stay the same. God is a radical life-changer. For some people, the change takes place more slowly or in different sequence than in others. The change is not always as steady or as consistent as we could wish, but those who pursue God cannot stay the same. God is love, God is true, God is righteous, and God is good. When we set our hearts on Him, our hearts are moved, pressed, shaped, broken, and crushed sometimes joyously and sometimes excruciatingly into His likeness.

They see things. People who pursue God have eyes that have been healed. They may look at the sky, a freshly mowed field, a squalid alleyway, the face of a child, or a stream of travelers at an airport, and suddenly their heart nearly bursts with joy or breaks with sorrow. They've just caught a glimpse of life and reality through God's eyes. Sometimes they can put it into words for others, and sometimes they simply treasure it in their heart or seek out a place to pray.

They experience suffering. The journey into God is not all trumpets and halos. We are imperfect, and we live in a broken world. Suffering is one of the marks of this present order, and believers are not exempt. Suffering is one of the ways God deepens our understanding, sharpens our sight and hearing, equips us to serve others, increases our joy, and makes us more like Himself. I do not know why it is so, but it just is—the path into God is painful. It seems those He has called into special closeness to His heart He allows to go through deeper sufferings. As A. W. Tozer once observed, "Before God can use a man greatly, He must first wound him deeply." The same thought is amplified by this unknown poet:

> When God wants to drill a man,
> And thrill a man,
> And skill a man
> To play the noblest part;
> When He yearns with all His heart
> To create so great and bold a man
> That all the world shall be amazed,
> Watch His methods, watch His ways!
> How He ruthlessly perfects
> Whom He royally elects!
> How He hammers him and hurts him,
> And with mighty blows converts him
> Into trial shapes of clay which
> Only God understands;
> While his tortured heart is crying
> And he lifts beseeching hands!
> How He bends but never breaks
> When his good He undertakes;
> How He uses whom He chooses,
> And with every purpose fuses him:
> By every act induces him
> To try His splendor out—
> God knows what He's about.

We must not let this frighten us or deter us from seeking Him. God's love holds us and sustains us, but we must be realistic. The journey into God is not for the fainthearted.

The realization that God uses suffering to refine us and make us more useful and beautiful certainly does not mean we ought to seek suffering. By no means! Rather, we must seek God and trust that He is able to use suffering—however painful, however confusing, however intense—to accomplish good things in us.

They experience confusion. This is an extension of the former observation. People who seek God diligently for a lifetime sometimes find themselves in gloom rather than light. Some call it "dry times," some call it "darkness," and some may have other terms. Like Job they will sit in ashes and wonder where God is and why He is silent. At such times God's laws do not seem to be working (or they seem to be working backward). God's promises seem to be suspended, prayers go unanswered, and God doesn't seem to be anywhere around.

I do not know all God's purposes for allowing confusing events. Some experience this as a time to deepen faith, others as a time to purify their hearts. Some come through it stronger, more beautiful, and more useful. Others demand answers from God or even turn away from faith. For some people, God's purposes for the experience become clear along the way. Others never do understand why, but conclude that God is answer enough. Job's friends were shocked to hear him express confusion about God and came to the conclusion that his righteous past was only a cover for sinfulness, which of course added to Job's confusion.

Many righteous people since Job's time have found themselves in similar confusion. Their circumstances don't seem to mesh with their understanding of God. Or they find their hearts to be painfully dull and unresponsive in spite of intense longing for God.

They love. Those who pursue God are pursuing the essence of love. They cannot progress in the journey without love, and they cannot progress without being changed into love. It is God's love that draws us into Him, and love is His number one instruction to us. He seeks us in love, and He calls us to love. We have been "so loved," and He wants us to be known by our love—for Him first and then for one another. Love for neighbor, love for the poor, love for the lost, and love even for those who hate us and make life difficult for us.

As Jesus says,

> "If you love those who love you, what credit is that to you? For even sinners love those who love them. And if you do good to those who do good to you, what credit is that to you? For even sinners do the same. And if you lend to those from whom you hope to receive back, what credit is that to you? For even sinners lend to sinners to receive as much back. But love your enemies, do good, and lend, hoping for nothing in return; and your reward will be great, and you will be sons of the Most High. For He is kind to the unthankful and evil. Therefore be merciful, just as your Father also is merciful."
>
> *Luke 6:32–36*

Learning to know God is a journey. As I stand pointing ahead, my hope is that in your heart a fire will be kindled that cannot be quenched, a yearning stirred that refuses to be quieted.

Nine centuries ago, Bernard of Clairvaux wrote a hymn that expresses this kind of yearning:

> Jesus, Thou Joy of loving hearts!
> Thou Fount of life! Thou Light of men!
> From the best bliss that earth imparts,
> We turn unfilled to Thee again.
>
> Thy truth unchanged hath ever stood;
> Thou savest those that on Thee call;
> To them that seek Thee, Thou art good,
> To them that find Thee, all in all.

We taste Thee, O Thou Living Bread,
And long to feast upon Thee still;
We drink of Thee, the Fountain Head,
And thirst our souls from Thee to fill!

Our restless spirits yearn for Thee,
Where'er our changeful lot is cast;
Glad, when Thy gracious smile we see,
Blest, when our faith can hold Thee fast.

WALKING WITH GOD

Following are activities for you to pursue further:

1. Both Moses and Paul, towering God-chasers from different eras, expressed a yearning near the end of their lives to know God. Study the context of each of these quotes to better understand what was in each man's heart.

    a. Moses pled, "You have said, 'I know you by name, and you have also found grace in My sight.' Now therefore, I pray, if I have found grace in Your sight, show me now Your way, that I may know You and that I may find grace in Your sight" (Exodus 33:12, 13).

    b. Paul cried, "That I may know Him and the power of His resurrection, and the fellowship of His sufferings, being conformed to His death, if, by any means, I may attain to the resurrection from the dead" (Philippians 3:10, 11).

2. Take some time to meditate on Jesus' discourses with His disciples the night He was arrested, as recorded by John in chapters 13–17 of his gospel. This section richly and poignantly shows us God's heart. Try making a list of everything Jesus said about His Father. Meditate on the list and let His Spirit talk to you.

3. One of the most distressing dimensions of acquaintance with God involves dealing with misconceptions. Sometimes these misconceptions are honestly held; sometimes they are held

emotionally long after the intellectual correction has happened. Some people, for example, find themselves drawn to Jesus while maintaining emotional aloofness toward God the Father. Barbara Kingsolver writes a fictional story about a missionary family to the Belgian Congo. The father preached a hellfire God in ways that not only missed the locals, but also spiritually sterilized his four daughters. His wife reflects:

> We sang in church "Tata Nzolo!" Which means *Father in Heaven* or *Father of Fish Bait* depending on just how you sing it, and that pretty well summed up my quandary. I could never work out whether we were to view religion as a life insurance policy or a life sentence. I can understand a wrathful God who'd just as soon dangle us all from a hook. And I can understand a tender, unprejudiced Jesus. But I could never quite feature the two of them living in the same house. You wind up walking on eggshells, never knowing which *Tata Nzolo* is home at the moment. Under that uncertain roof, where was the place for my girls? No wonder they hardly seemed to love me half the time—I couldn't step in front of my husband to shelter them from his scorching light. They were expected to look at him and go blind.[2]

a. Try to put in your own words the misconceptions reflected in this excerpt.

b. What are the most troubling misconceptions among Christians you know?

c. How are your perceptions? Do you have an emotional distinction between the Father and the Son? (This is not to suggest there is no distinction in function or person between the Father and the Son, but to say our misconceptions may cause us to be drawn to one but not the other.)

d. How do you think misconceptions about God can be corrected?

4. James Smith emphasizes the importance of knowing God in worship and worshiping in community. Believing that humans were made to worship God, and consequently we must get our lives back in line with our Creator to be fully human again, he writes:

> In a strange and terrifying sense, the vocation of being human requires utter dependence on God; the task of being a creature requires being ordered to the Creator. Gathering

as an answer to the call to worship is a displacement of any human self-confidence or presumption. Implicit in the very act of gathering is an understanding that human flourishing requires a dynamic relationship with the Creator of humanity; in short, worship is at the heart of being human.[3]

a. How does this understanding of God and relationship with Him structure our priorities?

b. Our acquaintance with God has a significant bearing on our view of those who don't know God, and it could take us to places good or bad. One of the inherent traps in learning to know God is to take on a spiritual snootiness, to assume that we are now "in the know" and unbelievers are unfortunately mistaken on every point. This is quite different from what should happen in true acquaintance with God, where we experience an indescribable and humbling realization of grace, an overwhelming sense of ongoing dependence, and a sincere compassion for those who still can't see Him or who waste their lives pursuing "that which is not bread." As you think of your own acquaintance with God, how has it shaped your view of those who don't know Him or who harbor misconceptions about Him? (In a later section, we will explore further the reality of our own imperfect understanding of God.)

Notes

1. Margaret Manning, "God's Hiding Place," *A Slice of Infinity*, daily e-mail devotional, Ravi Zacharias International Ministries, April 28, 2009.

2. Barbara Kingsolver, *The Poisonwood Bible* (New York: HarperCollins Publishers, 1998), 96.

3. James K. A. Smith, *Desiring the Kingdom* (Grand Rapids: Baker Academic, 2009), 165-166.

GOD IS HOLY

Holy, holy, holy is the LORD of hosts;
The whole earth is full of His glory!

ISAIAH 6:3

Give to the LORD the glory due His name;
Bring an offering, and come into His courts.
Oh, worship the LORD in the beauty of holiness!
Tremble before Him, all the earth.

PSALM 96:8, 9

He who is the blessed and only Potentate,
the King of kings and Lord of lords,
who alone has immortality,
dwelling in unapproachable light,
whom no man has seen or can see,
to whom be honor and everlasting power. Amen.

1 TIMOTHY 6:15, 16

To think rightly about God, we must know Him as a person, not as a specimen. A specimen is dissected; a person is appreciated. A specimen is laid out in parts; a person is known as a whole. A specimen is a subject to be studied and talked about; a person is to be known, loved, and befriended.

When we begin to talk about who God is, we must not approach Him as an interesting subject. We are not analyzing Him. We are not cutting Him into distinct parts. We are learning to know Him and love Him.

Our friends display strengths of personality and character that we learn to recognize and find endearing. We may speak gratefully of a friend's thoughtfulness because we've experienced that thoughtfulness or witnessed it being shown to others. Just to think of those incidents of kindness or encouragement warms our hearts. Speaking of an especially close friend or an especially meaningful interaction may move us to tears or to exclamations of delight or shouts of laughter.

As much as our friends warm us, move us, comfort us, and encourage us and much as we love them, they are imperfect. They sometimes fail us and disappoint us. Sometimes they forget us or badly misunderstand us. Still we love them.

As we begin to think about who God is, we must keep several things in focus. First, we are talking about a person. He lives. He thinks, He feels, He chooses, He plans, He acts, and He relates. When we talk about God's holiness or His love, we are not taking Him apart bit by bit in scientific analysis, but discussing how we have experienced Him and known Him in real-life interactions.

Second, when we think about God as a person, we are thinking about the perfection of personhood. He is whole and well-adjusted. He is the perfection of being. He never falls short. He acts in unfailing consistency with Himself.

As a person, God is transcendent. He blows all our circuits, passes all knowledge, and exceeds all boundaries and limitations that we may unwittingly place upon Him. As A. W. Tozer wrote,

> We must not think of God as highest in an ascending order of beings. . . . This would be to grant God

> eminence, even pre-eminence, but that is not enough; we must grant Him transcendence in the fullest meaning of that word. Forever God stands apart, in light unapproachable. He is as high above an archangel as above a caterpillar, for the gulf that separates the archangel from the caterpillar is but finite, while the gulf between God and the archangel is infinite. The caterpillar and the archangel, though far removed from each other in the scale of created things, are nevertheless one in that they are alike created.[1]

Because God is God, He is beyond and above us. But He is person. We can know Him, love Him, and grow in relationship with Him.

As we consider God's holiness and then His love and His other attributes, we will say things and think things that are true. But they will be true in the fullest sense only as we experience Him in these ways. For example, we may talk about "Honest Abe," but only those who interacted with Abraham Lincoln truly knew the man.

God is not dated. He was and is and He always will be. The whole point of this study is to learn to know Him as a person. When we truly know Him, we will want to fall at His feet in worship because this person is God.

† † †

God is holy. We will attempt to gather the courage to contemplate this holy God. When we are first introduced to God in the Bible, He is acting like God. He thinks and then speaks the world with all its life and laws into existence. He forms the first man and woman and provides them with a home and a few directions for what to do and how to care for it. He is God—good, benevolent, thoughtful, wise, and in charge, loading our existence with blessings rich and varied.

The coming of sin wrecks the good and beautiful world. This is an ugly part of the story, but it is in the context of this chapter of man's history that we best understand God's holiness. The concept of holiness is unmistakably imbedded in Genesis 3, though the word itself isn't mentioned.

The Hebrew word translated *holy* is borrowed from the butcher shop. It means literally "cut apart." As the butcher wields his knife, he removes the objectionable from the desired—the fat, the bone, and the organs from the meat. The remaining portion is choice, desired, and set apart. It is "holy."

The Hebrews used this designation for anything set apart for God because they understood their holy God to be set apart from everything else. He is the absolutely "other," unlike anyone or anything else. Because He is like no other and has no equal, nothing was to be used to try to represent Him. He is holy holy. Most holy.

In the story of the Fall, we understand that God is holy specifically because He is "other than" the fallenness of humans. He is other than the sinfulness in this present world order, and other than the deception and murderous intent of the enemy of all righteousness.

Between God and fallen man is a moral chasm. He is morally right; we are morally corrupted. Because He is moral perfection in Himself, all that He says and does is morally perfect. All that He thinks, decides, plans, and wills is holy, holy, holy, because He is holy. Because God is moral perfection, He is the measure by which we determine that all that is other than He is morally deficient.

If this were our whole understanding of God, or even our entire understanding of His holiness, we would despair. It is disconcerting, especially in our condition, to think of God as "other." Set apart in such holiness, He is inapproachable and remote.

We must not go wrong places here. Holiness is not priggishness. God does not piously fold His hands on the sidelines of life, frowning at every caper of humans and especially irritated when they enjoy themselves. He does not call men and women to sober faces and dull living for the rest of eternity.

Our holy God engages in the real world with His sleeves rolled up. He reaches across the divide. He puts His arms around miserable sinners and draws them to Himself. He speaks not in tones of cold command, but in words of hope and invitation. He beckons us to come. He takes people like Noah, Abraham, Jacob, and Samson into His plans. He bridges the divide. He speaks and acts toward redemption.

When God speaks of moral issues, He tells us what is right and what is wrong, and He doesn't fudge. Thou shalt, and thou shalt not. His commands are for our restoration and salvation. He speaks these commands out of the essence of His being. In Leviticus, for example, when God tells Moses what the Israelites were to do and what they were not to do, He frames the commands with the explanation, "I am the Lord," or "I am the Lord thy God" (see especially chapters 18 and following). He was not making an arbitrary list of rules, but explaining to His people how the moral perfection of His character should find expression in human existence. He was telling them what is in accord with His being and what is not in accord.

When God said, "Thou shalt not commit adultery," He was describing how His holy, righteous, and loving being would find expression in a marriage relationship. In such a situation, God would be faithful and committed, not treacherous and deceiving. When He said, "Thou shalt not steal," He was describing how His holy and good character would express itself in neighborly dealings. He would honor the person and possessions of others and seek their good, not their ruin.

God's holiness is not always pleasing to us. To our sinful hearts it sometimes stabs like lightning, beats upon us like a sledgehammer, or searches us out to the point of great embarrassment. Good men and women cringe before the holiness of God; sinful men and women die. We are sometimes terrified by the flashes of God's unveiled holiness. Lamenting the loss of a sense of God's holiness, Drew Dyck writes:

> When God shows up in Scripture, people cower and tremble. They go mute. The ones who manage speech fall into despair. Fainters abound. Take the prophet Daniel. He could stare down lions, but when the heavens opened, he swooned. Ezekiel, too, was overwhelmed by his vision of God. After witnessing Yahweh's throne chariot lift into the air with the sound of a jet engine, he fell face-first to the ground. When Solomon dedicated the temple, the glory of the Lord

> was so overpowering, "the priests could not perform their service" (1 Kings 8:11).
>
> New Testament types fared no better. John's revelations left him lying on the ground "as though dead" (Rev. 1:17). The disciples dropped when they saw Jesus transfigured. Even the intrepid Saul marching to Damascus collapsed before the blazing brilliance of the resurrected Christ.
>
> I understand why such accounts are jarring for us. They stand in stark contrast from popular depictions. . . . In Scripture . . . divine encounters are terrifying, leaving even the most stout and spiritual vibrating with fear—or lying face-down, unconscious.[2]

In those cowering moments, we might like to make God different. More like us. We'd like to change Him so He could say, "Thou shalt not commit adultery, except under great stress." Or, "Thou shalt not steal, except from corrupt governments or greedy corporations." We would like to change the reality of sin. We would like at least sometimes to call evil good and good evil.

We would especially like to change the consequences of sin so it wouldn't lead to death and wouldn't always bring sorrow and pain. But we could never make such changes without changing who God is. And if we could change who God is, He would no longer be good, holy, and true.

To understand holiness, we must understand that God defines holiness rather than the other way around. And that means holiness is good.

The old writers, even under the glare of a less gracious covenant, understood that God's holiness at the core was all we could desire or hope for. They spoke of the "beauty of holiness." It was not frigid or barren against a black-and-white landscape, but alive with radiance and glory.

Nathan Stone, commenting on God's holiness, says:

> It is in His transcendent holiness that the glory and beauty of Jehovah consist. In the great song of triumph

> sung by Moses and the children of Israel after their passage through the Red Sea (Exod. 15). . . the greatest tribute paid to Jehovah is in the words: "Who is like unto thee, O Jehovah . . . glorious in holiness." The cry of the seraphim, who veil their eyes in the presence of God's holiness, is "Holy, holy, holy, is the Lord of hosts": and then, "the whole earth is full of his glory." It is against the glory of God's holiness that all have sinned, for this is what Paul meant when he said: "All have sinned, and come short of the glory of God" (Rom. 3:23).[3]

God gave His people pictures, ceremonies, and illustrations to help them toward the truth. He asked them, for example, to build a place—a holy, holy, holy place. It was designed to appeal to each of the senses. In the scintillating light of the lamps, God's people saw glittering gold, decorative carvings, and multicolored weavings. They smelled the aromatic incense and the burnt offerings. They tasted the wafers and choice portions of sacrifice. They heard the bells, the ram's horns, and the psalms sung and played on a variety of stringed instruments. They felt the wetness of water and blood and rich anointing oil, as well as the warm priestly hands of blessing. At times they saw special flashes and revelations of glory—a fiery cloud covering the tent of meeting, Mount Sinai billowing like a furnace gone berserk.

This visual and tactile and aural display trumpeted something loud and clear. The holy God is beautiful beyond description. He is set apart in glory. There is no one like Him now or ever. He is light, loveliness, and grandeur beyond our wildest imagination. He stoops to using the best we know and understand to show us that our present senses simply could not take in the real glory.

God's holiness is the reason, the cause, and the foundation for all that is holy in this world. Because God is holy, the places He has chosen to reveal Himself are holy. Such common substances as stones, bowls, utensils, fire, oil, and furniture become holy. The people who follow God are likewise holy. In both covenants, God says to His people, "You shall be holy; for I am holy" (Leviticus 11:44; 1 Peter 1:16).

Looking at it this way, "Be holy" is not only a command, but also a pronouncement. Because God is holy, everything and everyone belonging to Him is set apart, reserved, and consecrated to Him for His good purposes. We must not remove the call to be holy from this command, but it is inexpressibly comforting to experience the great and gentle hands of holy God upon our heads as we believe in His Son and to hear the divine pronouncement: "Be holy, because I am holy!"

God calls us to dedicate our lives and our bodies to Him and in that dedication to view ourselves as holy—as belonging to Him. This does not call us out of this world, but aligns us to live in the world in the right way. Holy people eat. They work, they type, they garden, they change diapers, they make mistakes, they paint, they think, they dream, they sing—on and off key—in short, they enter into life in all its dimensions. But they are His. And because they are His, they are marked. In His eyesight, they stand out—choice, desired, set apart, holy.

WALKING WITH GOD

1. Consider these men and their encounters with God's holiness. What do these encounters show us about God's holiness? How did these events affect these people?
    a. Moses: "Take off your shoes!" (Exodus 3)
    b. Isaiah: "I am ruined!" (Isaiah 6)
2. Consider the descriptions of God's holiness in Psalm 29:2 and Psalm 96:9. What are your thoughts on the connection between beauty and holiness?
3. God's holiness stands in contrast to man's sinfulness. Read 1 Peter 1:13–16. After meditating on what he has to say, try writing a paraphrase.

4. Do you think God's holiness is understood and emphasized too much or too little in our day? What are the results of either imbalance?

5. Try writing to God your thoughts on His holiness. How does contemplation of His holiness affect your view of yourself? When you think about moving into deep and meaningful relationship with God, how do thoughts of His holiness affect you?

6. Does your concept of the holiness of God exclude beauty and joy? Or dull it in any way? Rethink. Try reading and meditating on Isaiah 35, perhaps in a variety of translations. This is a prophetic passage about the "Highway of Holiness" (v.8). List all the references to beauty and joy. This is an acquaintance with God that causes us to dance (or leap, if you prefer, or at least raise the corners of our mouths)!

Notes

1. A. W. Tozer, *The Knowledge of the Holy* (New York: Harper & Row Publishers, 1961), 75-76.

2. Drew Dyck, "How We Forget the Holiness of God," Christianity Today, May 20, 2014, http://www.christianitytoday.com/ct/2014/may/how-we-forgot-holiness-of-god.html

3. Nathan Stone, *Names of God* (Chicago: Moody Press, 1944), 101.

GOD IS LOVE

I bow my knees to the Father of our Lord Jesus Christ . . .
that He would grant you, according to the riches of His glory,
to be strengthened with might through His Spirit in the inner man;
that Christ may dwell in your hearts through faith;
that you, being rooted and grounded in love,
may be able to comprehend with all the saints
what is the width and length and depth and height—
to know the love of Christ which passes knowledge;
that you may be filled with all the fullness of God.

EPHESIANS 3:14,16–19

Beloved, let us love one another,
for love is of God;
and everyone who loves is born of God and knows God.
He who does not love does not know God,
for God is love.

1 JOHN 4:7, 8

Somewhere around the year AD 1050 a Hebrew poet by the name of Meir Ben Isaac Nehoria wrote the following lines:

> Could we with ink the ocean fill
> And were the skies of parchment made;
> Were every stalk on earth a quill,
> And every man a scribe by trade;
> To write the love of God above
> Would drain the ocean dry;
> Nor could the scroll contain the whole,
> Though stretched from sky to sky.

I've sung this song many times and have caught myself wondering at its hyperbole, trying to visualize it actually happening—every person writing a description of God's love and draining an ocean of ink in the process.

Truth be told, every person is a chapter of that love, written or unwritten, known or unknown. For the love of God has been poured out on human existence, every day giving us food, water, air, life, friends, and a thousand other blessings. He pours out those blessings not only on those who love Him, but also upon those who curse Him, ignore Him, neglect Him, and turn from Him. When the atheist uses logic and talents to try to disprove God's existence, he uses God's gifts to do so. When a bitter person curses God or blames Him for life's troubles, he vents his anger using air and energy given by God's good and loving hand.

Not only does God constantly lavish blessings on the unworthy, but He also has put Himself out for them—to the death. Paul says we should be dumbfounded by this kind of love. We can understand that a person would give his life for a family member or close friend. We would call him a good man and say his sacrifice was exceptional. But that God would die for us when we are His enemies seems incredible. What kind of love is this!

Almost nine hundred years after Nehoria wrote his poem, a businessman by the name of Fredrick Lehman went through a series of reverses and lost most of his material assets. The year 1917 found him working in a packing plant in Pasadena, California, struggling to understand God's purposes in his losses and wondering if God really knew him and loved him. One Sunday evening, Lehman listened to a sermon on God's love. Thoughts from the sermon kept coming to him the next day while he worked. Being something of a musician, he began to compose the lyrics of a hymn in his mind, and then at home he sat down to his piano and began to compose the music.

> The love of God is greater far
> Than tongue or pen can ever tell;
> It goes beyond the highest star,
> And reaches to the lowest hell.
> The guilty pair, bowed down with care,
> God gave His Son to win;
> His erring child He reconciled,
> And pardoned from his sin.
>
> When hoary time shall pass away,
> And earthly thrones and kingdoms fall;
> When men who here refuse to pray,
> On rocks and hills and mountains call;
> God's love, so sure, shall still endure,
> All measureless and strong;
> Redeeming grace to Adam's race
> The saints' and angels' song.

At that time a song was considered incomplete if it did not have at least three stanzas, and Lehman had trouble coming up with a third stanza. Suddenly he remembered a poem he had seen on a card. He found the card and noticed at the bottom the following story:

> These words were found written on a cell wall in a prison some 200 years ago. It is not known why the prisoner was incarcerated; neither is it known if the words were original or if he had heard them somewhere and had decided to put them in a place where

> he could be reminded of the greatness of God's love—whatever the circumstances, he wrote them on the wall of his prison cell. In due time, he died and the men who had the job of repainting his cell were impressed by the poem. Before their paint brushes had obliterated the words, one of the men jotted them down and thus they were preserved."

Imagine Lehman's delight when he found that the words of this poem fit the meter and melody of his new song perfectly. He published his song, using the prisoner's poem as his third stanza. More recently it was discovered that the prisoner's poem was a translation of the poem written in Hebrew by Meir Ben Isaac Nehoria, quoted at the beginning of this chapter. Not only had God arranged for the two sets of lyrics to come together, but He brought them from the pens of a Jewish Rabbi and a Christian businessman who lived almost nine hundred years apart.[1]

I tell this story, of course, to make a point. Much has been written and preached and sung and painted about the love of God. I wonder how many volumes of books and scores of music and paintings and sermons have been crafted. I wonder how much time has been spent meditating to formulate all that work.

God's love is. Like a gigantic mountain that dwarfs Everest and that no man or woman can scale, it is. But exactly because it staggers our thinking and dwarfs all our ideas of huge and defies our puny attempts to scale it, we can easily perceive it in our mind's eye as existing at a great distance—as something unattainable. In other words, all that truth doesn't mean much until we, like Lehman, find it breaking through our wretched problems in a personal encounter. We want to know that the great mountain of God's love is personal. We long for the comforting awareness that God actually knows us by name and cares for us as persons.

In this chapter I want to take us up the mountain. We won't get far beyond the lowest outcroppings, but I'm not so intent on reaching the summit as on pointing you in that direction. My hope is that somewhere along the way you will find yourself in some cleft, small or large, where the glory passes by and you hear God's voice, cover your face, and cry out in soul-deep realization: "God loves me!"

God is love.

In three simple words John states a truth so profound we are left with mouths gaping silently when we try to express it. "God is love" (1 John 4:8). He could have said, "God loves," or "God knows how to love," or "God is the best example of love," or even, "God is the best lover." All would have been true. But he said, "God is love."

Two things hit us. First, John is not simply describing something about God. Many biblical writers used adjectives to describe God—He is holy, good, righteous, and so on. And John could have said that God is loving. Again, it would have been true. But John uses a noun—love. God is something. He doesn't just "do" love or act in loving ways. God is essentially love. It is in His being, in the "molecules" of His divinity.

This answers a fundamental question about God's love to us. Because love is a relational characteristic, we tend to love what pleases us, what attracts us, what gives us joy; or maybe more specifically, *who* pleases us, attracts us, and gives us joy. Our love depends on the recipient. We tend to love people who love us.

God loves because God is love. Love is essential to His being. The sweetness and flavor of a ripe Golden Delicious apple is intrinsic to the apple's essential makeup. It is sweet and crisp and dripping with flavor because it is a Golden Delicious apple. It doesn't change its essence depending on who bites into the apple. A good man or a bad man, an adult or a child, a saint or a psychopath can bite into the apple, and it will be sweet and crisp to all the same because it is a Golden Delicious apple.

God is love. He sends His rain and sunshine on the fields of good men and criminals alike. He gives air and water to prostitutes and liars, as well as to those who sacrificially run a soup kitchen. Both moral people and twisted perverts are given life and talents from the loving heart of God.

This God is moved by human need. He is touched with our sorrow. He is saddened by our sin, by our record of poor choices, by our selfishness and lust and short-sightedness, by our insistence on charting our own course, by our refusal to come to Him, and by our attempts to rearrange the lines of morality to fit our interests.

This God is love. He acts in our interests even when we don't. He moves to engage us even when we walk away from Him. He loves this foolish, groaning, twisted world, but not because we are cute and cuddly and He just can't help it. He loves us because He is love. He loves us out of Himself in the face of our unlovable selfishness, stubbornness, and sin. God is love.

God defines love.

The second thing that strikes us in John's description of God is that since God is love, love is defined by Him, not by us.

Here we are up against a significant challenge. I will try to frame it accurately. God is love, and we are made in God's image. We are, consequently, lovers at heart. It is an essential element of our being to set our hearts upon, to yearn and desire and care about and seek relationship with and commit ourselves to . . . to what? To whom? By what means?

Ah, here we want to be our own gods. We want to determine for ourselves what and whom and how we love. We want to define love by our own yearnings, by our own loves, by our own desires.

As fallen beings, we are idolaters. We turn from our design. We turn from our Designer. His highest command to us is that we love Him. Our strongest counter-demand is that we have the freedom to love what we want (and because I am me, only I know what I really want). So we set our hearts on gods we can see and manage—on money or houses or lands or pleasures or travel or education or prestige or popularity or position or recreation or entertainment or gadgets.

We don't take into account that the object of our heart's greatest desire—the thing that gets our attention, holds our interest, takes our time, and receives our sacrifices—will shape our hearts. When we love money, money shapes our hearts. When we love pleasures, those pleasures shape our hearts. And when we love God, He shapes our hearts.

So let's get back to God. God is love.

This means love is defined by who He is and how He loves, not by who we are and how we love.

Just as we hang on tenaciously to the gods we love, so we hang on tenaciously to our understanding of love. (And because we have many gods, some opposites of each other, we also have many definitions of love, some with exactly opposite meanings.) Love, we think, is the sum of the feelings that race through us when we are having fun with our friends or when we are sexually aroused. Love is anything that makes me thrilled. Love is everything nice and pleasant. It gives me what I need and should also help me get what I want. We define love by our own gods and our own experiences. And we get angry when God isn't like our idols and when God doesn't give us what pleases us. In our childishness, we deny His love.

God is love, and God defines love. In whatever ways we think God hasn't been loving, whether toward us or toward others, we are either misjudging the event, as in blaming God for what He hasn't done, or misunderstanding love.

God is love. All that He does, He does in accord with Himself. When God cursed the earth, He did so in love. (Imagine a sinful world with no consequences, no trouble, no groaning, and no pain.) When God judges the world and purges it of its evil forever, He will do so in love. He cannot and will not act contrary to Himself. Ever! But we may misjudge Him to be unloving if we use our own understanding.

If we want to understand love, we must not think of it primarily as a quality. Love is in the person of God, and it is in relationship with God that we will understand love. To know God and to come into relationship with Him is to embark on an experience of love. We begin to understand love properly when we repent of our idols—when we turn in sorrow from the folly of devoting our hearts to anything other than God—and give to God our heart's devotion. God is love, and learning to know love begins with loving Him.

In loving relationship with God, we learn that He has acted in love from the beginning. Love moved Him in Creation, love moved Him in responding to Adam and Eve's sin, love moved Him in calling Abraham, love moved Him in choosing the nation of Israel, love moved Him in her destruction and exile, love moved Him in sending prophets, love moved Him in the Incarnation, love moved Him all through the ministry of Jesus, love moved Him in the death and resurrection of His Son, love moved Him to pour out His Spirit on the gathered disciples, love has moved Him and will move Him in all the centuries of human history, and love will move Him to wrap up all things to His glory through His Son Jesus.

Love is essentially reciprocal.

Love is relational by nature. As humans made in God's image, we feel the deep longing for another being, the tug for connection. Ironically, it is possible for that inner longing to be entirely one-sided. As long as love stays unexpressed, the other person may be completely oblivious to our desire for connection.

This has been the subject of many stories, some gut-wrenching in their intensity and others absurd, especially when a love-smitten guy is head-over-heels in the imaginary world of lovey-dovey and the one he loves is not only oblivious, but also quite different in reality from the princess she is assumed to be.

When love is actually extended from one party to another, it can either be accepted or rejected. When love is accepted, it has the potential to flower into the richness of a love relationship. When rejected, love either remains in that one-sided condition, longing for reciprocation, or sadly in many human relationships, it turns to hate and reciprocated rejection.

This is the great risk of love in a fallen world, and God has taken the risk of loving us when we were alienated from Him, offering us deep and eternal relationship. His love for us, immense and astounding as it is, does not actually reach its fullness until it is reciprocated. Deep and wide beyond all measure, poured out in incredible sacrifice through Jesus, God's love does us no good as long as we are dead in sin. You can give a dead dog the best food imaginable. You can shower it with attention and ear rubs and kind words. But a dead dog benefits nothing from such kind attention. Even so, until we respond to God's love, we cannot really know it.

God's love is voluntary and personal.

My illustration of the apple earlier captures only so much. Taken too far, it is a false analogy. An apple is delicious because it is an apple, and it doesn't differentiate between nice or nasty people because it has no mind, no will, and no feelings. It has no personality, and we can have no real relationship with an apple. Our experience with it, however pleasant, is short-lived and impersonal. We eat it and forget it.

God is not an apple. He is not helpless in His love for us. God's love to us is voluntary—He has chosen to love us, and His love calls us into relationship with Him. He has noticed us, turned His attention upon us, looked kindly and compassionately at our hopeless situation, and acted in our best interests at frightful cost to Himself.

His love for us is relational and dynamic. He has not only "so loved the world," but He knows and loves us as individuals. He knows us by name. He calls us into His family and urges us to explore our relationship with Him as sons and daughters.

When we first experience the personal love of God, it bursts upon our souls like an explosion of joy and wonder. *God has chosen to love me!* Our hearts experience no greater yearning than to love and be loved. This yearning lies at the core of our identity. Our deepest love defines who we are. When we love God, we learn that we are His—made by Him, chosen by Him, loved by Him, and belonging to Him forever. We become a member of God's people! This reality anchors the soul. We can face virtually anything when we are in His love.

God's love toward us becomes the source and definition of love from us. As we live in relationship with Him, our love grows. Our love takes on the characteristics of God's love—we become like Him. His love to us shapes us. Our love back to Him shapes us too. In relationship with this Person, we are restored more and more into the loving person He is and the loving persons He intends for us to be. The best way to grow in love is to live in a continual giving and receiving of the love of God.

Even as God is love, we are redeemed into the same image. Love becomes who we are—the essence of our person, not in isolation from God, of course, but in union with Him. As John puts it, "We love because he first loved us" (1 John 4:19, ESV).[2]

Love finds expression.

Love is essential to God and to those who live in relationship with Him. Love is not first something they do or say, but it is who they are.

Still, love finds expression. Love is always deeper than its expression, but love cannot exist without seeking to be expressed. It finds its way into our intentions, our plans, our desires, our actions, our words, and our mannerisms. "Many waters cannot quench love," Solomon wrote in his songs of love (Song of Solomon 8:7). And this is true whether it is the love of a man for a woman or the love of a human heart for its Creator.

When we love, we want to act and speak expressions of our love. Toward God, this is nothing short of worship. We want to express our devotion in lives given to Him, offered as "living sacrifices," as reasonable, fitting acts of worship (Romans 12:1). We want to speak our love—to put into words the joy and wonder of His love for us, and the adoration of our hearts for Him. We read the Psalms, sing the hymns, say the creeds, and our hearts leap up with an everlasting "Yes!" We also offer spontaneous words of love—testimonies, we sometimes call them. Or when we are walking or driving or sitting, sometimes the words burst from us unplanned. Love seeks expression!

Nothing is quite like knowing God's love in our hearts and experiencing our love coursing back from our heart to His. The divine "I love you" from Him washes over us and through us, calling from us a heartfelt and life-encompassing "I love You!" in response. Time stops as the heart of heaven and the responding hearts of clay shout expressions of love one to another.

But true love is not mere words. Nor is it only exhilarated feelings. True, it is heart-stoppingly enjoyable in those moments of worshipful bliss. But love lays life on the line. It is expressed powerfully and sometimes painfully in continued commitment when ecstatic feelings are absent. We love Him in the dry times, the painful times, the confusing times, and the dark times because His love to us is no less then. If anything, when we hurt, when we cry, when life is black and tumbled, His love grows deeper. For us, love has the potential to grow deeper during difficult times.

Love for God, like love in marriage, encompasses all of life. There is no time, no location, no experience when love from Him does not reach us and enrich us (whether we can sense it or not) or when our love for Him does not quiet our hearts and steady our steps. We are joined to Him by love in an eternal union that water, fire, flood, angels, demons, and nothing else in all creation can separate.

Love is easiest to express when it is clearly felt in the heart. Such expressions of love are wholesome and good. They have the feel of authenticity. But sometimes we don't feel it in the heart. Sometimes we may actually feel other than loving toward God. We may feel frustrated or confused. It is all right to be honest with our contrary feelings. They often are clues to deeper needs in our hearts, and sorting through those feelings in God's presence can bring us into richer understanding of who He is.

On the other hand, we must not give way to our unloving feelings. Under the push of popular psychology, the pendulum has swung from ignoring feelings to validating all our feelings and encouraging unbridled expression. It seems that the danger of squelching our emotions and the value of being tuned to our feelings have both been overplayed to the point of not only letting our feelings hang out without any discretion but also validating any emotion-driven expression as real. In human relationships this can result in relational homicide, and in our relationship to God, it can lead people to a false sense of honesty and even honor at their freedom to "beat up on God" when things aren't going their way, which can be most of the time.

It seems to me there must be a healthy place between the extremes of venting every feeling we have in the interests of honesty with God and stifling our honest struggles. Here the Psalms provide us with a raw model. Those who wrote the psalms were not afraid to ask God hard questions. They did not turn back from expressing surprise, hurt, even anger about the difficult events and people in their lives. But such psalms almost invariably have a turning point, a "But God" juncture. At that crossroads, the psalmist turns from expressions of frustration to expressions of faith and love that sound like this: "But You are my refuge, my rock, my defense, my strength, my deliverer; and I will praise Your name forever." The psalmist seems to be willing to do this even before he experienced deliverance.

This is loving God by faith.

We do not need to see the good hand of God to know it is there. We do not need to hear God's comforting voice or experience His deliverance to believe that His heart is toward us, that He loves us intensely, and that we are in His care.

Our expressions of love to God are appropriate when we feel close to Him, when we have enjoyed a special time with Him. But our love for God must be bigger and deeper than responding to Him when we feel His love. Expressing love from our heart to His when we do not understand Him, when He seems distant, when life is hard, and when He has allowed desperate situations from which there seems to be no recovery is far more true to the love He has given us than merely venting our "honest feelings."

True love begs to be expressed. If God's love surpasses our love, is it not reasonable that expressions of that love will sometimes run counter to our natural inclinations? If you feel like giving God a verbal punch and priding yourself in your honesty, instead you might think about telling Him what is true about His love for you—that it is deeper and higher and wider than you can describe. You will likely find it more inspiring to describe His love for you than to tell Him what is true about your feelings in the moment.

God's love is transforming.

God's love reaches into the wretched lives of people who can't get up in the morning when they ought, who harbor nasty thoughts about other people, who sometimes say unkind words to the people they love best, who pray mostly selfish prayers . . . yes, God's love reaches out to ordinary people like you and me every day. He invites us to be part of His people. He extends His love to us to arrest our selfishness and transform us into loving sons and daughters who increasingly bear His image.

John is sometimes called the Apostle of Love because the love of God is so prominent in his writings. After telling us God is love and describing how God's love was extended to us in Jesus, John calls us to love. "Beloved, if God so loved us, we also ought to love one another" (1 John 4:11).

God's love poured out on us makes us truly the "beloved," those who have been lavished by divine love. This love produces an "ought to." By receiving His love, we become obligated to love—God first, but others also. John carries this forward both as an obligation and as an inevitable result. He concludes this unparalleled exposition of "God's love causing our love" with a bold but unqualified assertion: "If someone says, 'I love God,' and hates his brother, he is a liar; for he who does not love his brother whom he has seen, how can he love God whom he has not seen?" (v. 20).

God's love to us produces our love for God. "We love Him because He first loved us" (1 John 4:19). But God's love is also the source of our love for others. Some of the Greek texts do not have "Him," and the text simply reads, "We love because He first loved us." God's love to us is not static. It is alive and productive. It changes us. It cuts to the heart of our selfishness, sends us to our knees in repentance, and transforms our inner character. God's love coming into us remakes us to be more and more like Him.

I was walking the streets of New York City with friends, heading toward Washington Park to share the Gospel, when I heard a commotion behind me. I looked around and saw a man running after us on the opposite side of the street, yelling and waving for us to stop. When he caught up with us, he wanted to know if we were Christians. I assured him we were, and his face broke into a broad smile. He was a Christian, too, he said. Then he began telling me his story.

Bob was not a Christian when he married. The mother of the woman he married wanted her daughter to marry someone else. She eventually convinced her daughter to divorce Bob and marry the other man. Understandably, Bob turned bitter. He was angry with his wife for desertion and betrayal, but he hated his mother-in-law. I do not remember all the details, but sometime after his marriage fell apart, Bob heard the good news of Jesus and received Him into his heart.

Now here's the remarkable part. Bob told us that some months after becoming a Christian, he suddenly realized while he was praying that he was no longer bitter toward his wife. He found himself praying for her, wanting her to experience the life of Jesus too. Then he paused and said, "And you know what? Sometime later I was praying again, and I realized that I no longer hated my mother-in-law. I wanted her to be saved too."

God's love in Bob's life changed the natural bent of his heart. It turned his hateful heart into a heart that loved even those people who had hurt him most deeply. That is the nature of the love of God. It transforms. It gets into the roots of our being. It refuses to let us be okay with our selfishness. As someone put it, "God loves us as we are, but too much to let us stay that way."

WALKING WITH GOD

1. Consider the following examples of people in the Bible encountering God's love. What do these stories show us about the love of God? How did these events affect or change these people?
    a. God's love for Israel (Deuteronomy 7:6–15).
    b. Hosea: Loving his unfaithful wife illustrates God loving unfaithful Israel (Hosea 1–3).
    c. Sinful woman: Jesus said she loved much (Luke 7:36–50).
2. What is your favorite song about the love of God? Sing it to God. Try reading/singing the following hymns to God:
    a. "Great God, Indulge My Humble Claim"
    b. "I Would Love Thee"
    c. "I Am Thine, O Lord"
    d. "When I Survey the Wondrous Cross"
3. In spite of the assurances of God's love for us, we tend to doubt it. Take some time to explore your own doubts. In what ways or under what circumstances have you doubted God's love? Can you describe your greatest inner objection or what stands in your heart as an obstacle to believing and receiving the love of God?

4. How do you know God loves you? How have you experienced God's love? Meditate on this for a time, and write the responses that come to your mind. Let your heart worship.

5. Read Romans 5:6–10. Paul's comments on the incredible love of God shown toward us as sinners should leave our jaws gaping. Then Paul takes it to the next level. Read this in a variety of translations. Think how Paul experienced God's love in waywardness, and then as a redeemed son of God. Try writing your own paraphrase of the thoughts in this passage.

6. Perhaps you can identify with this anonymous writer, reflecting on the development of his understanding of God's love.

> Growing up in Western culture, I was taught to value empirical understanding and individual choice. My Christian heritage gave me an understanding of God as Creator and Sustainer of life, as the one over everything, ordering world events toward His ultimate purposes and as the one to whom we will someday give account. My particular Christian sub-culture emphasized right living, hard work, honesty, and community. That is, our sub-cultural community was a distinct and separate group in a wicked society and even a distinct and separate group in the larger Christian community, which was generally viewed as weak and errant.
>
> The view I had of God and His people was profoundly simple and relatively safe.
>
> As I grew older, I learned that many of my fears about God were based on misconceptions. I knew God's love in a doctrinal sense—I could quote the verses and say the right things about His love, but to learn to know His love in a personal sense has been a heart-warming and soul-breaking experience. The shift has been something like staring at a black-and-white photo, and finding it take on color; the characters come alive, and I can actually move into the scene in living experience.

7. Try describing your own story. How has your understanding of God's love changed and grown as you have learned to know Him? What misconceptions have you had? How has God worked to correct those misconceptions? What part of God's love do you know to be true but still struggle to grasp and "know" in your heart?

Notes

1. This story is told in Alfred Smith, *Treasury of Hymn Histories* (Montrose, PA: Heritage Music Distributors, Inc., 1982), 247-248.

2. The difference between the newer translations ("We love because he first loved us") and the older KJV, which the NKJV follows ("We love him because he first loved us") is a difference in the Greek texts, not a difference in how the text is translated. Both texts make true statements.

GOD IS GOOD

I would have lost heart, unless I had believed
That I would see the goodness of the Lord
In the land of the living.

PSALM 27:13

The earth is full of the goodness of the Lord.

PSALM 33:5

Some years ago I listened to a friend give a series of talks on the life of Joseph to a group of students. At the beginning of his lectures he said, "If I could convince you of one thing true about God that you would retain for the rest of your life, that one thing would be that God is good."

I was surprised. We live in a relationally challenged culture, and it is common to hear preachers describe the struggle we have believing God loves us. Then they address God's love as foundational to all right understanding about God. I'm not saying they are wrong. It just surprised me to hear someone talk about God's goodness as being so pivotal to our faith.

I don't think we need to try to determine which quality of God is most important. In any given situation, any one of them can be most important, and to single them out may actually contribute to a fragmented understanding of God. He is, of course, good and loving and holy and immutable and just and everything else God-like in full measure all the time.

I do believe God's goodness is a life-giving beacon of hope in a fallen world. In our particular cultural circumstances, His goodness is both commonly doubted and desperately needed.

God is good.

When we think about God's goodness, we tend to think along moral lines. God is good in contrast to bad. This is not a totally wrong way to think about God's goodness. It simply doesn't include everything that the writers of Scripture mean, or even most essentially what they mean, when they describe God as good. As A. W. Tozer says,

> When Christian theology says that God is good, it is not the same as saying that He is righteous or holy. . . . The goodness of God is that which disposes Him to be kind, cordial, benevolent, and full of good will toward men. He is tenderhearted and of quick sympathy, and His unfailing attitude toward all moral beings is open, frank, and friendly. By His nature He is inclined to bestow blessedness and He takes holy pleasure in the happiness of His people.[1]

God truly is "inclined to bestow blessedness," or in less staid language, He is crazy generous. It is in Him to be a giver, to nurture, to make happy, to prosper, to burst human hearts with pleasure. This is what we mean when we affirm that God is good. And although God's goodness is intrinsic to Him, it is known in His myriad acts of kindness every day, in His good works from beginning to end. When God made the world, every day's work was good, good, good. He was giving, providing, making happy, and preparing blessing upon blessing for us even before we were here.

When God calls humans to Himself, He is exercising His goodness. When He rescues us, when He hears us, when He talks to us, when He answers our prayers, when He intervenes, even when He disciplines us, God is good. His words and actions toward us give life, bring us pleasure, and are intended for our absolute best.

God's goodness is abounding.

"The earth is full of the goodness of the Lord" (Psalm 33:5).

When God created the earth, He was exercising His goodness, filling it with all sorts of surprises and pleasures for us to discover and enjoy. These pleasures caress (sometimes assault) our senses continually.

We taste His goodness.

- Buttery, salted sweet corn, or your favorite vegetable: asparagus, peas, green beans, lima beans, baked beans, carrots, beets, spinach, broccoli, squash . . .
- Slurpy watermelon, or your favorite fruit: cantaloupe, peaches, apples, cherries, mangoes, strawberries, raspberries, blackberries, elderberries, pears, pineapples, bananas—and you can have that fruit chilled, fresh, dried, sweetened, mixed, or baked in dumplings or pies or served with ice cream.
- Potatoes, any way you like 'em—baked, mashed, fried, grilled, boiled, roasted—and served with butter, cheese, sour cream, slaw, or gravy.
- Nuts: cashews, pecans, almonds, filberts, macadamias, Brazil nuts, or peanuts—roasted, salted, mixed, or chopped and sprinkled on a variety of other foods.
- T-bone steaks, chops, wings, breasts, ribs, roasts, duck, mutton, or wild game—done rare or medium or well; barbequed, baked, roasted, or fried, and served with your favorite mouth-watering (or lip-burning) sauces.
- Seafood: All kinds of fish—cod, mackerel, trout, salmon, walleye, grouper, catfish, sunfish—plus scallops, shrimp, lobster, crabs, oysters, clams, and for the exotic experience, squid or eel or . . . And again, you can have that grilled, pan-fried, baked, battered, salted, or even sushi style.
- And all the grains—wheat, oats, barley, rice, spelt—milled in a variety of ways and kneaded and baked into a thousand kinds of breads, cakes, muffins, crusts, cereals, buns, croissants, and pastries.

Ooh boy! When God filled the world with food, He said, "That's good!" And over and over, every day we affirm it with oohs and aahs and pleasurable sighs as we taste His goodness. The earth is full of the goodness of God!

We smell His goodness. Walk into the kitchen when any of the above foods is baking or sizzling or boiling, and you will begin to drool. The very smell of food sets the digestive process in motion. But food is not all we smell. How about freshly mown hay; a springtime morning, rows of lilac bushes (or honeysuckle), the approach of rain, a washed and lotioned baby, roses by the dozen, a flower garden or a greenhouse, silage early on a summer morning, burning candles, perfume, sanded lumber (oak, pine, walnut), a young child's sweaty head, coffee brewing in the morning, the sea breezes, a horse barn, a spice and herb shop, or perhaps even a skunk on a sultry day?

Aah . . . the earth is full of the goodness of God.

We see His goodness. It's all around us—in sunsets and sunrises, canyons, hills and mountains, streams and rivers and lakes and seas (flowing, falling, cascading, crashing, billowing), trees (single giants, saplings, snow-laden, forests, fall colors), pasture lands and crops, gardens lush or groomed, clouds (Oh my! Thunderheads, all sizes and shapes, black and billowing, white against a blue sky, wispy horse tails, soft gray blankets curled around the hills or snuggling down in the hollows), fish in coral reefs (blue and yellow and orange and red, marked with black and white stripes and spots). We stumble onto and study animals that amaze us with their antics, cunning, adaptation, or skill—a beehive, an ant colony, a beaver's house, a frolicking river otter's mud slide, a hummingbird nest, butterflies and birds in amazing configurations of color, stars, shooting meteors in a black sky, the interior of a flower (color, pollen, anthers) the silvery underside of maple leaves caught in the breeze . . . Every day our eyes take in this kaleidoscope of colors, designs, and movements that delights us and stirs us to awe and worship—unless we are so occupied with getting to places on time or doing drivel that we are oblivious to all this visual goodness.

We hear His goodness. How many sounds of water are there? How many sounds of the wind? And music—my, oh my! We've made the instruments of music, of course, but He gave us the gift of sound and hearing and the ability to express and perceive the meaning and to appreciate the beauty and complexity of chords and progressions made with wind instruments, strings, percussion, and the human voice. Listen to the sounds of birds trilling, whistling, warbling, shrieking, chirping, and hooting! Or the sounds of insects—crickets, locusts, cicadas, and bees. Spring peepers and frogs on a summer night! The sounds of our pets barking, meowing, and chirping. Barnyard sounds—cattle, horses, chickens, ducks, sheep, roosters in the morning. Our ears are constantly massaged with God's goodness.

We can feel His goodness. We touch—we feel smooth, soft baby skin, rough bark of trees, a warm mug of hot chocolate or coffee or tea, pinpoints of cold as snowflakes drop on an upturned face, heart-stopping waves of romantic feelings, an arm around our shoulders when we are sad, the texture of crisp apples or piping hot mashed potatoes and gravy, the comfy feeling of familiar shoes or sandals or favorite clothes, a kiss, a hug from an ecstatic child, the pit-of-the-stomach thrill on a huge swing, a wriggling worm on our palm, bare feet in the grass, splashing through a mud puddle, warm summer rain, cool mist of fog in the face on an early morning bike ride, weightless floating on the surface of a pool, changes in water temperature when diving into a lake, hot shower and toweling off after a sweltering day, hot sauce burning the tongue and throat and lips, the satisfaction of scratching an insect bite, holding the hand of a friend, a deep muscle massage, my spouse's fingers idly strolling through my hair, the recliner after a hot shower, drowsy content after a delicious meal . . . In so many ways we feel God's goodness.

Okay, I've belabored the point. But God designed us to experience His goodness, to be reminded every day that He delights in making humans happy, comfortable, and surprised with joy. That's God. He has filled the earth with His goodness.

But we must understand two important points. First, God is not good because of these things. He is good. These scrumptious, beautiful, and invigorating blessings come from His goodness, but they do not make Him good. Second . . .

The earth is also filled with evil.
Some years ago I read a detailed account of the Holocaust as told by a Jewish historian. The savagery, prejudice, hatred, betrayal, and horror of those grim years are beyond our comprehension. He told of an incident where SS troops mercilessly evacuated a Jewish ghetto, including the hospital. Soldiers threw babies out of upper-story windows, and soldiers outside caught them on bayonets until their guns were too slippery to grasp.

If this were an isolated era in human history, it would be one thing. It's not. The brutality of humans to each other seems to be continuous, from small neighborhoods to big cities to nations all around the world: Rwanda, Uganda, South Africa, Serbia, Beirut, and the Gaza Strip, to mention a few in the recent past. Or look at what our European ancestors did to Native Americans, or what white farmers did to their black slaves in the South. The earth is full of evil.

The evil of the world easily obscures the goodness of God.

Multitudes have stumbled here. So many things are wrong in the world—injustice, oppression, cruelty, treachery, broken promises, ruined lives, displaced people, torture, plundering, rape, annihilation. These set off the urge for revenge, and a whole new round of violence and evil and death ensues.

The same senses that taste, smell, see, hear, and feel the goodness of God are sometimes assaulted with pain and screams, the sight of torn and bleeding bodies or starving infants, and the noxious odors of decaying flesh. The true accounts of sieges and battles and bombings and butchery and torture of human bodies stagger our ability to make sense of human existence. Over and over we ask in shock, "Why?"

When the blood and pain and suffering come closer home, we readily lose sight of (sometimes savagely discard) God's goodness. That's what my friend at the beginning of the chapter was getting at. Because we live in a world of evil that seems more sinister with each new invention, we will personally encounter evil or tragedy. Such evil easily overwhelms us. The shocked "Why?" when we read about other people's sorrow quickly turns to an accusing "Why?" directed at God.

How can a good God permit such evil?

Either He is not good, the logic goes, or He is not God. For no good man would stand by and watch the atrocities of other men go unchecked if he had the power to stop it. So God is either not good or He is not God.

We are up against another dimension of God here—His righteousness. I find it amazing how quickly people judge God as unrighteous when they encounter overwhelming trouble. I'll get to this later, devoting a chapter to God's righteousness, but let me note here that we can't discuss God's goodness without referring to His righteousness.

I want to reiterate that God is not good "because." We are not proving anything when we point out His goodness in the pleasures we experience from His good hand. And since He is not good "because," neither is He bad "because." If we try to establish God's goodness through the good things in the earth, we will soon stumble in this; for if luscious food proves He is good, then indiscriminate suffering proves He is not good.

When we experience overwhelming evil, our doubts about the goodness of God are based on several false assumptions.

We assume, for example, that a good God cannot allow trouble—at least, not terrible trouble—and still be good. To our way of thinking, He is not good when He allows bad things to happen. Furthermore, we assume that when terrible things happen (especially to wonderful people), God is not running the world right. He is unfair, unjust, unwise, unable, or un-something—He surely isn't acting godly at all. Some declare this conclusion outright and leave the faith (such as Charles Templeton, a one-time fellow evangelist with Billy Graham). Probably few of us have not entertained these nagging thoughts or feelings at some point.

Another assumption we make is that our experiences and our conclusions about them constitute the whole picture. We live life a moment at a time, one event after another. "Time," someone has said, "is what keeps life from happening all at once." So we move from an up to a down, from one conviction to its opposite. Consequently we must base our lives on something more durable than personal experience, something more than a mouthful of food and something more than a tragedy.

God is good, and no evil in the world (not even all the combined evil in the world) can change that reality.

Evil may cloud our vision. Holy men and women have struggled here, so we must not conclude we are terrible people because we have terrible doubts. The truth is that no evil on earth can diminish the goodness of God even slightly.

When we encounter evil and when we are overwhelmed with unanswered questions about tragedy, sickness, pain, or death, we must anchor our hearts on several realities. The first one I've already said, but I'll repeat it and then move on:

1. God is good no matter what our circumstances. Bad circumstances in my life cannot alter God's goodness any more than cloud cover can alter the reality of the sun.
2. The goodness of God is demonstrated through His gracious blessings and through delivering us from evil, but it is even more powerfully demonstrated through redemption from evil.
3. Trouble offers the opportunity of learning to know God's goodness in deeper ways.
4. Redemption is experienced as we exercise faith in God.

God's goodness is demonstrated through redemption.

This is an amazing window into the goodness of God. He is able to turn any earthly sorrow into the very thing that moves forward His good intentions. He is able to bring testimonies of grace out of tragedy, joy out of sorrow, riches out of loss, resurrection out of death.

The analogy of the sun being unaffected by clouds makes one point about God's goodness but misses another. True, the sun is unaffected by clouds, but it is ninety-three million miles away from us on a rainy day. Our God is not good from a distance. He comes among us. He enters our sorrow. He promises to be with us. Jesus came into human tragedy, felt our sufferings, experienced our thirst, bled with our wounds, wept over denial and betrayal, and cried out in anguish at being left to die. When we go through these sorrows, God brings Himself into our experiences—His love, His joy, His grace, His peace, His fullness, His healing, His forgiveness, and His life.

God is a redeemer. Stories of horrible tragedy abound, but for every kind of human sorrow, there are multiplied stories of redemption. Because God is with us and God is good—kind-hearted and compassionate and desiring to bring us to peace and fullness—He can bring inexpressible goodness out of terrible badness.

As a young boy, my father was healthy and full of life. All that changed at the age of ten when a baseball thrown by a schoolteacher hit him in the back of his neck. For the rest of his life he walked on crutches or was pushed in a wheelchair. That very limitation, however, opened to him the world of books. One of those books was the Bible. I knew my father as a man who knew God and loved people. My father died when I was a teenager, but I have no recollection of hearing him complain. In fact, I grew up thinking I was privileged to have a father who walked with crutches. He was not a perfect man, but he was a man of character.

I have many memories of people coming into our home to ask my father for help—a young man in medical school facing challenges to his faith, a young widow whose husband took his own life. God used the injury that robbed my father of a healthy body to equip him to bless and encourage others.

We see God's good hand redeeming people from tragedy in the lives of Biblical characters—in the rejection and abuse Joseph suffered, in the grief and hardship of the young widow Ruth, in the injustice and adversity David went through, in the unspeakable calamities of Job, in the threats and danger suffered by Daniel and his three friends. God is a redeemer—He is able to cause human tragedy to bring suffering believers into incredible encounters with His goodness.

We can never predict how God will work, and in the middle of the sorrow, we are in no position to judge Him. But if we trust Him, He is able to work everything, whether big or small, complicated or impossible, into good for us.

We must trust Him to experience His goodness.
"I would have lost heart," wrote David, "unless I had believed that I would see the goodness of the LORD in the land of the living" (Psalm 27:13). Faith enables us to keep going when tragedy is overwhelming, and it releases the hand of God to work good things in our lives.

On Saturday, August 30, 2003, Robert and Melissa Rogers and their four children were traveling home from a wedding when they were caught in a flash flood on I-35 near Emporia, Kansas. A wall of water washed their stalled minivan off the highway and tumbled it like a matchbox downstream. Robert kicked out a window hoping to rescue his family, but he, his wife, and their oldest daughter were sucked out into Jacob's Creek, which had turned into a raging river. Robert survived, but his entire family perished.

At a press conference two days later, while searchers were still looking for Melissa, Robert offered the following statement:

> Let me start by saying that "God is God, and I am not." The biggest question we have right now is, "Why?" We don't have an answer, but we have faith and trust in the sovereignty of God. . . . [He then talked about what he had experienced that terrible night.]
>
> Nevertheless, "It is well with my soul." Even though we're literally walking through the valley of the shadow of death, God's peace that passes all understanding is guarding our hearts and our minds. There is peace in knowing that all four of our children are now with our Lord and Savior, Jesus, in heaven. There is peace in knowing that God is still sovereign and that God is good—all the time. What the devil meant for bad, God will somehow turn to good.
>
> I feel God reminding me to be still and know that He is good.[2]

The goodness of God is the reality that enables us to go on when life doesn't make sense. But we must trust His goodness. Faith when we cannot understand, when we are overwhelmed with trouble, is not blindness or stupidity. It is sanity. It would be senseless to trust our own judgment at those times.

Notice that Robert *expressed* his faith in God's goodness. He did not understand what God was doing. He was honest enough to acknowledge his unanswered "Why?" But he confessed with his mouth what he knew was true about God. That confession encouraged his own heart and the hearts of others.

In 2004, Rogers left his job and launched *Mighty in the Land Ministry*. He tells his story of faith to thousands of people every year and enlarges on a theme he introduced in that first press conference, where he said, "If there's anything positive that can come from this terrible tragedy, it is to treasure the importance of families . . . to savor every single minute with your spouses and children. Hug and kiss them every day—every morning and every evening. Tell them over and over how much you love them. Snuggle with them at bedtime. Place your hand on their heads and bless them every day."[3]

Gracia Burnham, who spent more than a year in captivity with her husband—he was shot to death and she escaped—wrote this in response to Robert's story: "Being tried and tested changes your outlook on life. You no longer take things for granted: a hug, a meal with those you love, companionship. Thank you, Robert, for encouraging us to see every day and every blessing as a precious treasure. Thank you for the motivation you've given us to live our lives to the fullest with no regrets."[4] Gracia's own story, recounted in her book *In the Presence of My Enemies*, has had a similar impact.

Stephen Saint, whose father Nate was murdered by Auca Indians, was in a spiritually and emotionally low time during a trip to Africa. By "chance" he decided to visit Timbuktu, a remote African village (yes, the place actually exists). In a setting hostile to Christianity, he was able to meet a Christian who invited him into his house. This Christian talked about the rejection and harsh persecution he faced from his family. "But," he went on, "it helps me so much to know that others have suffered and even died for Jesus. Especially, I've been encouraged by the story of a man who has the same surname as you have—Saint. His story has often kept me going." Stephen was nearly overcome with the realization that his father's death—the very cause of his own current struggles and doubts—was actually the cause of this man's strength. To think that God had arranged for him to meet this man in Timbuktu to speak into his doubts!

Annie Johnson Flint was orphaned at an early age. When she was a young adult, her foster parents both died as well. A few years later she began to experience crippling arthritis that left her an invalid. She supported herself (barely) for nearly forty years by writing poetry for greeting cards. Her solid faith in God's goodness in spite of painful and difficult circumstances is one of the most common themes of her poetry. Ironically, she seldom referred to her own suffering either in conversation or in her poetry. She said she wrote her poems with the difficulties of others in mind.

Here is an example:

I Will Not Doubt

I will not doubt though all my ships at sea
Come drifting home with broken masts and sails.
I shall believe the Hand that never fails
From seeming evil worketh good for me.
And though I weep because those ships are battered,
Still will I cry while my best hopes are shattered,
"I trust in Thee!"

I will not doubt, though all my prayers return
Unanswered from the still white realm above.
I shall believe it is an all-wise Love which has
Refused things for which I yearn;
And though at times I cannot keep from grieving,
Yet the pure ardor of my fixed believing
Undiminished shall burn.

I will not doubt though sorrows fall like rain
And troubles swarm like bees about a hive.
I shall believe the heights for which I strive
Are only reached by anguish and by pain.
And though I groan and tremble 'neath my crosses,

I yet shall see through my severest losses
The greater gain.

As I was writing the final chapters of this book, my mother passed away. She was eighty-two years old. The last years of her life, her speech and mobility were crippled by strokes. In her Bible I found the above poem and learned from my sister that it had been one of her favorite readings through the forty-three years of her life as a widow.

We live in a world of evil and trouble, sorrow and senseless tragedy. But God is incredibly good. He has entered our world. And He lives to turn tragedy on its head for His glory. Over and over He weaves together the tangled strands of trouble to show His unspeakable goodness to those who believe in Him.

I have proved nothing in this chapter. I have only attempted to point to what is true. God is good. I close with a very old poem from George Herbert, whose life spanned from 1593 to 1633. Although the language and spelling are old style, it offers a timeless perspective.

The Pulley

When God at first made man,
Having a glasse of blessings standing by;
Let us (said he) poure on him all we can:
Let the worlds riches, which dispersed lie,
Contract into a span.

So strength first made a way
Then beautie flow'd, then wisdome, honour, pleasure:
When almost all was out, God made a stay,
Perceiving that alone of all his treasure
Rest in the bottome lay.

For if I should (said he)
Bestow this jewell also on my creature,
He would adore my gifts in stead of me,
And rest in Nature, not the God of Nature:
So both should losers be.

Yet let him keep the rest,
But keep them with repining restlesnesse:
Let him be rich and wearie, that at least,
If goodnesse leade him not, yet wearinesse
May tosse him to my breast.

WALKING WITH GOD

1. Consider the example of Habakkuk in his struggle to understand the goodness of God.

   a. Chapter 1: Habakkuk is in anguish over the sins of the Israelites. Then he must prophesy that God will use the proud, pagan Chaldeans, who were more wicked than the Israelites, to punish Israel. Habakkuk is appalled—how can a good God do this? After meditating on Habakkuk's questions, write out questions you have had about God's goodness.

   b. Chapter 2: After his anguished questions, Habakkuk says he will stand and wait for God's answer. Try to put in your own words God's response to evil (from Chapter 2). Can you find comments from Jesus that parallel God's words to Habakkuk? What does it do for us to know that the recompense to evil is in the hands of a righteous and true God?

   c. Chapter 3: Habakkuk talks to God. What does he request? What does he say about God? In the closing verses, Habakkuk states his faith. Put it in your own words. Paraphrase it to fit your situation or to address the questions you raised in the exercise above.

2. The psalmist says the earth is full of the goodness of the Lord (Psalm 33:5). Explore how you have experienced the goodness of God in each of the following ways:

   a. In nature.

   b. In health/sickness.

   c. In friendship/relational emptiness.

   d. In provision.

   e. In sacrifices.

f. In protection.

g. In trial.

3. We may struggle to believe God is good when our circumstances are bad. Consider the following Bible characters. For each of them, describe a time in their experience when they might have doubted God's goodness.

    a. Joseph

    b. David

    c. Ruth (or Naomi)

    d. Daniel

    e. Paul

4. Often when we know the "end of the story," we see how God really proved to be good, though the person involved may not have seen it at the time. For each of the above characters, tell how God showed His goodness.

5. Describe times in your life when you have doubted God's goodness. In light of the many examples of God's work in the lives of His people, what should be our response when we are tempted to doubt His goodness? If you are struggling currently to see God's goodness, try writing out what you see as an appropriate response to God.

Notes

1. A. W. Tozer, *The Knowledge of the Holy* (New York: Harper & Row Publishers, 1961), 88.

2. Robert Rogers with Stan Finger, *Into the Deep* (Carol Stream, IL: Tyndale House Publishers, Inc., 2007), 62-63.

3. Ibid., 62.

4. Ibid., opening comments.

GOD IS FAITHFUL

Through the Lord's mercies we are not consumed,
Because His compassions fail not.
They are new every morning;
Great is Your faithfulness.

LAMENTATIONS 3:22, 23

God is faithful,
by whom you were called
into the fellowship of His Son,
Jesus Christ our Lord.

1 CORINTHIANS 1:9

We need to talk about faith. To talk about faith, we need to talk about our situation. We live in a world of sin. It's all around us. The most damaging reality of sin is that it has gotten into us as well. We are sinners. We are bent on going our own way, even when we've been told the right way—sometimes especially when we've been told the right way. We want to be our own boss, make our own choices, and live our own lives. To our way of thinking, we are being more authentic when we do as we want rather than doing as we are told. We also think we are more free when we can do as we please.

If this all seems old hat, just hold on.

Sin is damning. Sin goes against everything God is. When we sin, we are not simply disobeying what God has said, we are violating who He is. God is life. God's laws and commands are statements about how to live His life, how to align our lives with His and function as we were designed.

When God tells us to do something or not to do something, He is telling us something about Himself—how His character finds expression in word and action, what is in accord with who He is, and what is a violation of who He is. He is also telling us something about us—how we were designed to function and how we were not designed to function.

When we do what God tells us to do, particularly when we do so in loving relationship with Him (which is the most important part of what He tells us to do), we are aligning our lives with the reality of God. Made in His image, we are becoming who we were intended to be.

When we disregard what God tells us, we are saying something is fundamentally wrong with God. In addition, we are doing violence to who we are. It is like trying to live contrary to the laws of the universe, like living on a diet of hallucinogenic drugs and declaring we are seeing and thinking straight.

God is life. God is the life-giver. God's ways are life-giving when they are pursued in passionate relationship with Him. Aligning ourselves with Him, especially after going our own way, is finding and coming back into life.

Believing in our drugs does not make them healthy for us; disregarding God and His ways is the road to death. There simply is no life outside God. There may be existence in separation from Him, but it is the existence of suffering and death, of sickness and dysfunction, of rot and decay, of hallucination and stupidity (sometimes brilliant stupidity), of separation and alienation, and of everything that leads to death.

The truth is that we don't take sin seriously. We can know it is wrong, we can despise it in other people, we can talk about it rightly in Sunday school, but we do it anyway. We don't believe God. Our unbelief gets us in trouble again and again. When we sin, we do not believe in God. We believe in ourselves, in our reasons, in our plans. We believe our way is better than God's way.

We are deceived, of course. On a sin kick. Sin leads to death, never to life.

There is one way out of sin and its consequences. It is the way of faith.

Faith starts with believing God is. It then affirms what God does and says. Faith is obeying God's commands, saying *yes* to God's will, affirming God's works, and amen-ing God's character. It is aligning our lives—our own words and actions—with the life and person of God.

In the convoluted labyrinth of sin, the way of faith is the way out. It is the way to pass from death to life. "Most assuredly [said Jesus], he who hears My word and believes in Him who sent Me has everlasting life, and shall not come into judgment, but has passed from death into life" (John 5:24). To put it bluntly, we won't get out of this world system alive without faith in God.

To be faithful, then—full of faith—is to believe God again and again.

Life is filled with tests to our faith. When we repent, turning from our way into God's way, we have made an important start. We see God's light. We experience God's life. We sorrow over the folly of our sin. This is faith—acknowledging our way was wrong and His ways are right.

Then the tests to our faith begin. We hit a problem—a loss, a hardship, sickness, unexpected bills, demands of people, or a strained or broken relationship. These problems put us in a spiritual fog. We can't see clearly. The same God we praised with such joy yesterday seems distant today. His ways don't seem to work. His instructions in such times can seem irrelevant, even unreasonable.

This murk is a test to our faith, though not necessarily sent as a test of faith. It's just the way a fallen world is—full of tests. Trials, we often call them. Our faith is being tried. Will we continue to affirm in our hearts the reality of God when we don't understand Him? Will we continue to do what He says even when it seems pointless? Will we trust Him when He says *no* to something we really want to do or to something we really want Him to do?

Believing in God again and again is being faithful.

Now, I've taken a long time to talk about what it means for us to be faithful for two reasons. First, because we use this term for God, even though some things are not the same. God doesn't live in spiritual fog. He doesn't exercise faith as we do. But God does act and speak in accord with who He is again and again. He never violates who He is. He "believes" in Himself no matter what the situation. He never acts contradictory to Himself. He keeps His word. He speaks truth. He acts with compassion. He does what is right. We can count on Him every time because God is faithful. As Moses put it,

> He is the Rock, his works are perfect,
> and all his ways are just.
> A faithful God who does no wrong,
> upright and just is he.
> *Deuteronomy 32:4, NIV*

The second reason I spent time looking at what it means for us to be faithful is that God's faithfulness in the Bible is often discussed and praised against the backdrop of our unfaithfulness (see Psalm 78 for an extended example). Arthur Pink, writing in the first half of the twentieth century, said:

> Unfaithfulness is one of the most outstanding sins of these evil days. In the business world, a man's word is, with exceedingly rare exceptions, no longer his bond. In the social world, marital infidelity abounds on every hand, the sacred bonds of wedlock being broken with as little regard as the discarding of an old garment. In the ecclesiastical realm, thousands who have solemnly covenanted to preach the truth make no scruple to attack and deny it. Nor can reader or writer claim complete immunity from this fearful sin: in how many ways have we been unfaithful to Christ, and to the light and privileges which God has entrusted to us! How refreshing, then, how unspeakably blessed, to lift our eyes

above this scene of ruin, and behold One who is faithful, faithful in all things, faithful at all times.[1]

Because God is faithful, we can count on Him.

Let's think a bit more about God's faithfulness. The Hebrew word translated *faith* or *faithful* means literally "firmness," and thus it is used to refer to that which is established or secure, a certainty. Because God is faithful, He is the one thing we can be sure about.

In a world of sin, finding such certainty makes us "unspeakably blessed," as Pink says. Most things we experience are not very certain—the economy, the political scene, our jobs, our health, our relationships, our possessions. Meet any old friend after twenty years of being apart, and see how much has changed!

Think of significant events that changed history—the Reformation, the American Revolution, the Civil War, the Depression, the World Wars, the crumbling of the Berlin Wall, the Gulf Wars, and 9/11. In each of these events, people lived and struggled and planned and yearned and prayed desperately. And from every one of these events come stories of faith—and of God's faithfulness.

In 1929 when the U.S. stock market crashed, the economy went into a nosedive from which it took years to recover. Millions of men lost their jobs, and multiplied thousands lost their farms and businesses. Some committed suicide. But likely from your own grandparents and great-grandparents come stories of God's provision and care. I wonder how many times when I was young I heard old people recall those times. They got quiet, almost reverent. "We didn't have much. We worked hard. But we never went hungry. And we were together as a family."

Hitler invaded Poland in 1939 and began to set up the Third Reich, which included annihilating Jews, Gypsies, blacks, and mentally handicapped people. On May 10, 1940, German forces swept into the Netherlands. In these terrible times, Corrie ten Boom hid Jews in her home, trusting God to provide for their needs and protect them from the German troops. God answered many prayers, providing food beyond their expectations and giving direction in dark and uncertain situations.

Then one night when Corrie was sick, German soldiers stormed their house and slapped Corrie to wakefulness, demanding answers she refused to give. Corrie, her sister Betsie, and their elderly father Casper were imprisoned, but the Jews they were hiding were not found. Casper died in prison. Betsie died in the Buchenwald death camp from overwork and malnutrition. Because of a "mistake" by a prison record keeper, Corrie was released. In view of these horrendous trials experienced by God's faithful people, was God still faithful? Was He acting consistently with Himself?

We are mistaken to think God's faithfulness shields us from all loss, hardship, sickness, or distress. No, it is in those very experiences we learn that God is faithful, the one certainty we can count on in a treacherous, changing, and broken world. He is watching over His own even when—especially when—they are in terrible circumstances. Read Corrie's story in *The Hiding Place*, and over and over we see that God was watching over them, acting in goodness, compassion, and righteousness, but often above and beyond what they could see in the moment. There are countless other stories of God's children experiencing His faithfulness: Michael Sattler in *Pilgrim Aflame*; Gracia Burnham in *In the Presence of My Enemies;* Jim Elliot and his fellow missionaries in *Through Gates of Splendor,* to name only a few.

Because God is faithful, He does not change under pressure.

God's faithfulness assures us that God does not change. It is because God is faithful that we can count on His love to be constant, His righteousness to be the same in every age, His character to be immutable day after day, generation after generation. Our fathers trusted Him, and we can trust Him. Believers in China, El Salvador, Australia, and the United States find the same God with the same character—kind, compassionate, just, holy, merciful, inviting, warning, calling, working His intentions. Situations change. Settings are radically different (Wall Street, slums, cities, small towns, far north, deep south, down under), but God is the same.

God's people not only run into problems, but they also sometimes create problems. The Israelites, who had experienced God's miraculous deliverance from Egypt, grew hot and hungry in the desert sun and grumbled and complained against Him. They were outright sarcastic with Moses: "Were the graves not good enough in Egypt? Did you think this hot sand would make a better cemetery?" Instead of having grateful hearts for what God had done, their hearts hardened into unbelief.

Any normal human leader in such a test—especially one with unlimited power—would have smacked the Israelites into outer space or made them eat wormy food three times a day for a week. Over and over they came up against difficulties and refused to believe God, choosing instead to mutter, vent their unbelief, and even turn to other gods for help. God performed miracle after miracle—fresh manna every morning, quails from the sky, water from a rock—to show them they could count on Him.

Through the era of the judges, their darkest time as a people, they turned away from God repeatedly, bowing down to poles and trees and carved images, mingling worship with depraved sexual acts, and offering their babies to the gods. When the consequences of their sin became unbearable, they turned back to God, asked for forgiveness, and begged for deliverance. Again and again God raised up saviors for them and rescued them from their drunken unbelief.

Under the kings, things went better for a couple of generations. Then the kingdom split. Israel in the north made no pretense of following God; Judah to the south had an up and down, on and off relationship with God. Things really went south with King Manasseh—oppression, killing, exploitation, sorcery, child sacrifice, sun worship, idols, and sacrifices to false gods right in God's temple—and God finally gave them over to their enemies. Assyria destroyed and scattered the northern kingdom, and then Babylon razed the walls of Jerusalem, sacked the temple, and carried off all but a few of the poorest into captivity.

Through this whole story of the unfaithfulness of God's people, God continued to act consistent with Himself. He had promised to bless the world through Abraham, to rescue His people out of Egypt, to lead them into the land of Canaan, to establish them as a people, to punish them when they went astray, to scatter them among the nations if they forsook Him, but to bring back a remnant and still fulfill His promise of an ultimate Savior. God did exactly what He said He would do because God is God and He always acts consistent with who He is and what He says, no matter how bad the circumstances. He doesn't become someone else under pressure.

Jeremiah was a prophet in the decades before Judah was completely destroyed. He witnessed the stubbornness of the last kings. He was imprisoned as a traitor during the siege because he, under God's direction, had encouraged the Jews to surrender to the Babylonian army. He watched with horror as King Zedekiah's sons were slaughtered and King Zedekiah's eyes were gouged out. He witnessed the walls of Jerusalem being torn down, the temple being demolished, the sacred furniture and utensils being wrapped up and carried off by Gentile hands, and the people he knew and loved being driven like animals down the long road to Babylon.

Jeremiah wrote a lament that moans and wails like a broken violin.

> The roads to Zion mourn
>   Because no one comes to the set feasts.
> All her gates are desolate;
>   Her priests sigh,
> Her virgins are afflicted,
>   And she is in bitterness.
> Her adversaries have become the master,
>   Her enemies prosper;
> For the Lord has afflicted her
>   Because of the multitude of her transgressions.
> Her children have gone into captivity before
>   the enemy.
>   *Lamentations 1:4, 5*

Even as Jeremiah's heart is crushed with sorrow, he recognizes God's faithfulness in what He has done. God has done what is consistent with Himself—what is right and true, what is in accord with His commitment to those who love Him and believe in Him, and what squares exactly with what He had promised to do. Jeremiah knows if it were not for God's faithfulness, they would have been toast in the hands of their enemies. There would have been no hope at all.

Remember my affliction and roaming,
    The wormwood and the gall.
My soul still remembers
    And sinks within me.
This I recall to my mind,
    Therefore I have hope.
Through the LORD's mercies we are not consumed,
    Because His compassions fail not.
They are new every morning;
    Great is Your faithfulness.
"The LORD is my portion," says my soul,
    "Therefore I hope in Him!"
The LORD is good to those who wait for Him,
    To the soul who seeks Him.
It is good that one should hope and wait quietly
    For the salvation of the LORD.
        Lamentations 3:19–26

In the destruction of His people, in allowing the Assyrians and the Babylonians to ruin their land and take them captive, in scattering them among the nations, God was still right. He was still keeping His word, still committed to their ultimate good, still watching over those few who believed in Him, still guided by a good and compassionate heart. Under test, under provocation after provocation over centuries, God is faithful to who He is. Jeremiah, even with his heart wrenched by witnessing horrible atrocities, found courage, comfort, and hope in the faithfulness of such a God.

Because God is faithful, we are always in His care.

One of the very practical expressions of God's faithfulness is the consistency of His care for His people. God demonstrates His faithful care in a variety of ways. For example, we depend on the "laws of nature" all the time—rain and sunshine to grow our crops, decomposition to fertilize the soil, pollination, photosynthesis, gravity, electricity, laws of motion, and seasons. These "ways" of the earth and air and living things and chemicals are kept going by the faithfulness of God. We can count on them being the same from day to day and season to season. We don't have to learn a different set of laws each year.

What a blessing this is in different arenas of learning—surgery, horticulture, industry, pharmacology, physics, astronomy, and culinary arts! Imagine if we could not count on salt, sugar, iron, or wood to act the same every day! What if refrigeration preserved foods one day and spoiled them the next? Every day we are nurtured and sustained because God faithfully causes the earth to "act the same."

God's people also experience God's faithful care through the circumstances and events of life. We are constantly in need and often in trouble. We've got daily food to provide, weekly schedules to meet, monthly bills to pay, jobs, children, health, and vehicles that break down at inopportune times. And several times a day we get into predicaments that put us in a sweat. Any one of these needs or predicaments can send our faith into a tailspin. Then we cry out to God.

Sometimes we manage to pray a really good prayer, but many times it's just a desperate yelp on the run. Over and over, the Lord provides for us in these events of life—if we let Him! Too often we try to work through this muck and trouble on our own, getting frustrated and short-tempered with people in our way, muttering and complaining about how hard we have it, and frantically fretting and figuring and fretting some more.

God invites us to bring our needs to Him. When we pause in His presence, talk to Him about our frustrations, and lay the impossible situations before Him, over and over we can experience His faithful care. The prayer-and-share times in the weekly gatherings of God's people are often filled with testimonies of how God met us in the daily hassles of life with a change of events, extra cash, words of encouragement from a friend, protection in a danger zone, or a verse or song that ministered to a harried heart. And through the fog and clutter, we are reminded that God is faithful.

Because God is faithful, He keeps His word.

In the early days of the church, many Jewish people believed in Jesus as the Messiah, resulting in much conflict and misunderstanding between the "old order" Jews and the new groups. Some of the new believers were thrown out on their ears. They lost their properties and inheritances, and were shamed and abused. At times these young followers of Jesus became discouraged, wondering if He really was the Messiah, and they considered giving up.

An early church leader (we don't know for sure who) wrote a letter of encouragement to these struggling believers. In his letter he repeatedly points them to Jesus and to the "better things" Jesus has brought to those who believe in Him—a better sacrifice, a better high priest with a better ministry, a better covenant based on better promises!

In chapter 10, he urges them to take advantage of the new provisions and enter into God's presence "through the veil" that was torn open in the death and resurrection of Jesus. And then he says, "Let us hold fast the confession of our hope without wavering, for He who promised is faithful" (Hebrews 10:23).

Yes! This God is faithful to keep His word.

The Father has made a new covenant with His people, signed with the blood of His Son and sealed with the stamp of His Holy Spirit. Here are the specific promises of the covenant:

1. I will put my laws in their minds and write them on their hearts.
2. I will be their God, and they shall be My people.
3. All shall know Me, from the least of them to the greatest of them.
4. I will be merciful to their unrighteousness, and their sins and their lawless deeds I will remember no more. (See Hebrews 8:8–12.)

When God makes promises, we can count on Him to keep His word. Today we receive the Holy Spirit into our hearts, transforming us and causing us to walk in ways of love and joy and peace above and beyond what the Old Testament law required. We experience a personal relationship with God. We do not need to go to a particular location or go through a mediating priest to know God. We are drawn into His family as sons and daughters, and He tells us to call Him "Papa." We experience the regular forgiveness of sins because God is faithful. "If we confess our sins, He is faithful and just to forgive us our sins" (1 John 1:9). You'd better believe it—God keeps His word!

Surrounding these terms of the covenant are many other promises. Here's a sampling paraphrased for our time:

"Put the kingdom of God first—living like Jesus—and I'll see to your food and clothes" (Matthew 6:33).

"When you are distraught and bone-weary with life and trouble, come to Me, and I'll blanket your heart with a calming peace like you've never dreamed of" (Matthew 11:28, 29).

"Whoever gives up anything for Me, whether big things or little, properties or relationships, the eternal blessings he or she receives in exchange will make those sacrifices look like nothing" (Matthew 19:29).

"Faith in Me resulting in a living relationship will be so satisfying it will seem like you are at a perpetual banquet" (John 6:35).

"The hearts of those who live in loving relationship with Me will be like artesian wells, with kindness and joy and goodness erupting from them everywhere they go" (John 7:38).

"I personally know and I'm committed to those who belong to Me, and with My life in them, they can neither die nor be destroyed by anyone, ever" (John 10:27, 28).

"I'm going back to My Father to prepare an eternal home for each of you, my followers, and I will return to escort you to your personal quarters with us forever" (John 14:2, 3).

"When you fully believe in Me and order your life that way, you will do the same kind of things I do and more. The Father will be absolutely delighted by how much your lives resemble Mine. In that oneness with Me, ask the Father for whatever you need, and nothing will be impossible" (John 14:12–14).

"Love Me and obey Me, and you not only receive the overflowing love of the Father on all your life, but My Father and I will make your heart our permanent residence" (John 14:23).

"Go about helping everyone who believes in Me to actually follow Me, and I will stand by you and assist you and empower you as long as time keeps going. Count on it, I will never, ever abandon you" (Matthew 28:18–20).

All these promises come directly from the heart of Jesus. It is so easy to live as though this world system with its sin and ruin and decay is the only reality. The truth is that Jesus is the Son of God. He "is the same yesterday, today, and forever" (Hebrews 13:8). Jesus began a new era in which He calls us to live with our eyes open to the reality of God the Father, God the Son, and God the Holy Spirit, alive and unchanging and fully able to carry out His word to those who live in His reality. Jesus inaugurated a kingdom that runs counter to the kingdoms of this world.

These promises of God in Jesus are for those who wrap their arms around Him and refuse to let go, for those who live in the truth of His presence. We must not take them out of context to build our own kingdoms and make our lives slick and sleek. These are God's promises to those who lovingly follow Jesus and are committed to bringing about His intentions on the earth.

Jesus has promised to bring in an era of righteousness and to overthrow the present system of sin. He calls us to live as He lived, rejecting and resisting the system of sin, already living in the new reality of the coming kingdom of righteousness, mercy, kindness, and goodwill to all. He calls us to live in the hope of the new era because we trust Him to keep His promises.

And Jesus Himself becomes the guarantee, the absolute yes, the forever-settled Amen of everything God has promised. In the words of our good brother Paul to early Corinthian believers, "As God is faithful, our word to you was not Yes and No. For the Son of God, Jesus Christ, who was preached among you by us . . . was not Yes and No, but in Him was Yes. For all the promises of God in Him are Yes, and in Him Amen, to the glory of God through us" (2 Corinthians 1:18–20). God has bound Himself to doing what He said.

If your heart has grown weary, if you have wondered if it is worth continuing on, listen again to the words of that early Jewish writer: "Let us hold fast the confession of our hope without wavering, for He who promised is faithful"! (Hebrews 10:23). God keeps His word. Oh, yes!

WALKING WITH GOD

1. Study the following examples of God's faithfulness—His commitment to keep His word.

    a. God promised to bring the Israelites out of Egypt and into Canaan. He said, "I have surely seen the oppression of My people who are in Egypt, and have heard their cry because of their taskmasters, for I know their sorrows. So I have come down to deliver them out of the hand of the Egyptians, and to bring them up from that land to a good and large land, to a land flowing with milk and honey" (Exodus 3:7, 8). Consider what obstacles stood in the way of God bringing the Israelites out of Egypt (not only among the Egyptians but also among God's people), and how God removed those obstacles to fulfill His promise. Consider all God did to bring the Israelites into Canaan according to His word.

    b. Through Moses, God promised blessings on the Israelites if they obeyed Him and curses if they forsook Him. "Behold, I set before you today a blessing and a curse: the blessing, if you obey the commandments of the Lord your God which I command you today; and the curse, if you do not obey the commandments of the Lord your God, but turn aside from the way which I command you today, to go after other gods which you have not known" (Deuteronomy 11:26–28). Can you give examples of God's faithfulness to each part of this promise?

    c. Jesus said, "I will build my church, and the gates of Hades shall not prevail against it" (Matthew 16:18). List some of the obstacles the early disciples faced. List some of the challenges and troubles the church has faced through history. In your estimation, what is most amazing about the fulfillment of Jesus' words?

2. What are your favorite stories (biblical or otherwise) that demonstrate the faithfulness of God?

3. William Ames said, "Faith is the virtue by which, clinging to the faithfulness of God, we lean upon Him, so that we may obtain what He gives to us." Under what conditions have you struggled most to believe that God will keep His word?

4. What particular promises of God have been anchor points for you? Which promises do you have most difficulty believing?

5. The New Testament writers frequently refer to God's faithfulness. These references urge us to trust God and live faithfully. To encourage your heart, take some time to look at the context of each of these references to God's faithfulness.

   a. 1 Corinthians 1:9. "God is faithful, by whom you were called into the fellowship of His Son, Jesus Christ our Lord." This is set in Paul's introductory remarks in his letter to an immature church that was torn by factions, fouled by immorality, and crippled by members seeking personal glory rather than the good of the group.

   b. 1 Corinthians 10:13. "No temptation has overtaken you except such as is common to man; but God is faithful, who will not allow you to be tempted beyond what you are able, but with the temptation will also make the way of escape, that you may be able to bear it." Paul emphasizes the importance of being true to God and not being disqualified by failure.

   c. 1 Thessalonians 5:24. "He who calls you is faithful, who also will do it." Paul assures these new believers of God's ability to make them holy and to preserve them until the coming of Jesus.

   d. 2 Thessalonians 3:3. "But the Lord is faithful, who will establish you and guard you from the evil one." Here God's faithfulness stands in contrast to those, even religious people, who oppose believers. God is fully able to keep His people.

   e. 2 Timothy 2:13.
      "If we are faithless,
      He remains faithful;
      He cannot deny Himself."
   This is part of a poetic and eloquent defense of the faithfulness of God.

   f. Hebrews 2:17. "Therefore, in all things He had to be made like His brethren, that He might be a merciful and faithful High Priest in things pertaining to God, to make propitiation for the sins of the people." Jesus' humanity was essential to His mission of shattering the enemy's powers and redeeming (absolutely) believers.

   g. Hebrews 3:2. "[Jesus] was faithful to Him who appointed Him, as Moses also was faithful in all His house." Moses was a faithful servant in all but the disobedience at the rock. Jesus is the faithful Son of God in every way, so we'd better pay attention to what He has said.

h. Hebrews 10:23. "Let us hold fast the confession of our hope without wavering, for He who promised is faithful." This entire letter is intended to urge believers not to give up or lose heart. Here that encouragement is solidly anchored in God's promises and the surety that He keeps His word.

i. Hebrews 11:11. "By faith Sarah herself also received strength to conceive seed, and she bore a child when she was past the age, because she judged Him faithful who had promised." Sarah, along with her faithful husband Abraham, trusted God's ability to do what He said, in spite of her initial incredulous humor at the thought of having a baby at ninety years old. She believed the impossible.

j. 1 Peter 4:19, NIV. "So then, those who suffer according to God's will should commit themselves to their faithful Creator and continue to do good." The subject is suffering for doing good. God's faithful presence enables believers to meet unspeakable injustice with a good attitude, forgiveness, kindness, and a continuing commitment to doing good.

k. 1 John 1:9. "If we confess our sins, He is faithful and just to forgive us our sins and to cleanse us from all unrighteousness." Our propensity to sin would overwhelm us if not for the reality that when we come to God in true penitence, He is faithful to His promise to forgive—no matter how often or how grievous our sin.

6. In addition to the above, we have a number of references to the faithfulness of Jesus in John's Revelation (see Revelation 1:5, 3:14, 19:11).

7. Through the centuries, many Christians have found that expressing their trust in God is an important part of growing their faith. Saying what is true about God is a way of strengthening our confidence in Him. This is not a matter of making up truth, but of affirming what is true. If I am standing on a solidly built observation deck hundreds of feet above a city and feeling queasy about my safety, I can tell myself what is true: this platform is well-built, I won't fall, and I can enjoy the sights. Hopefully those truths will calm my anxiety. I'm not making up truth; I'm simply affirming it.

   Even so, when circumstances make us theologically queasy, it is a good practice to talk truth to our souls: "God is over this situation. He knows me thoroughly, and He is fully able to take care of me if I trust Him." Think about troubling situations you are facing, and write out truth about God and His promises that you can trust. (Note: I have followed this practice for years, writing many prayers and expressions of my faith in God in difficult times. Actually, many of the psalms start with descriptions of trouble that change to expressions of trust. Try it yourself.)

Notes

1. Arthur Pink, *The Attributes of God* (Swengel, PA: Reiner Publications, 1968), 47.

8

GOD IS RIGHTEOUS

Righteous are You, O Lord,
And upright are Your judgments.
Your testimonies, which You have commanded,
Are righteous and very faithful.
Your righteousness is an everlasting righteousness,
And Your law is truth.

PSALM 119:137, 138, 142

Let the field be joyful, and all that is in it.
Then all the trees of the woods will rejoice before the Lord.
For He is coming, for He is coming to judge the earth.
He shall judge the world with righteousness,
And the peoples with His truth.

PSALM 96:12, 13

When we set out to explore the righteousness of God, we run into an immediate hitch—our sinfulness. This is no small problem. We were made in God's image with the ability to know right and wrong, but we barely had our feet under us before we gazed at the tree of the knowledge of good and evil and set about getting such knowledge our own way. The Fall left us with open eyes and closed hearts, a very dangerous moral dilemma.

God is merciful. He continues to pursue us, but the interchange of a righteous God with people of a twisted mind makes for a terrible dance. It has not always been pretty. We cannot explore His righteousness without taking into account our sinfulness. It's like trying to study the stars from an underwater lab. Even after we are redeemed we don't always see properly. We will explore this in greater detail later, but throughout the study of God's righteousness, you will see how our sinfulness pushes and pulls at our perspective, skewing and blurring our vision.

To get us started, let's meditate on Psalm 36. In the opening lines, the psalmist contemplates the wicked, drawing a strong link between their wicked ways and their disregard for God.

> An oracle within my heart concerning the
> transgression of the wicked:
> There is no fear of God before his eyes.
> For he flatters himself in his own eyes,
> When he finds out his iniquity and when he hates.
> The words of his mouth are wickedness and deceit;
> He has ceased to be wise and to do good.
> He devises wickedness on his bed;
> He sets himself in a way that is not good;
> He does not abhor evil.
> *Psalm 36:1–4*

The wicked person, in other words, lives according to his own desires. If a sinner wants to cheat—in business, in marriage, in friendship—he does so without regard to who God is or what He has said. He typically has his own standard of decency, but if he wants to lie or slander, he is his own authority. He thinks and plans how to do what he wants, and as the psalmist put it, "There is no fear of God before his eyes."

We who want to live righteously can be discouraged by the overwhelming wickedness and the regular disregard of God in the world. Sometimes we wonder what the point is of living for God, especially if we are having a hard time and the ungodly seem to be enjoying themselves. Sometimes we are tempted to think life would be more fulfilling if we, like the wicked, could live just to fulfill our own desires.

Righteousness—doing what is right—can look so restrictive to us. Or depending on the lighting, it can look boring, backward, prudish, old-fashioned, too difficult, or too costly. But after gazing at the life of the wicked, the psalmist fixes his eyes on the Lord and revels in who God is:

> Your mercy, O Lord, is in the heavens;
> Your faithfulness reaches to the clouds.
> Your righteousness is like the great mountains;
> Your judgments are a great deep;
> O Lord, You preserve man and beast.
> How precious is Your lovingkindness, O God!
> Therefore the children of men put their trust under the shadow of Your wings.
> They are abundantly satisfied with the fullness of Your house,
> And You give them drink from the river of Your pleasures.
> For with You is the fountain of life;
> In Your light we see light.
> *Psalm 36:5–9*

Against the backdrop of a wicked world, the beauty of God's character blazes like an exploding sun. God is a "fountain of life." His love, His faithfulness, His righteousness, and His justice are radiant with pure goodness and glory. We can hardly imagine a world in which everyone lived in full accord with God's character! But it certainly would not be boring or backward or prudish.

Like the psalmist, we must remind ourselves that God's righteousness is joined in perfection with all that He is. His righteousness is not separate from His love, His mercy, or His faithfulness. Even as His righteousness is loving and merciful, so His love and mercy are altogether righteous. God never acts righteously independent of His other attributes, nor does he act in faithfulness or judgment or love independent of His righteousness.

When God loves, He loves righteously. When God passes judgment, His decisions are absolutely right. When God shows mercy, when God forgives, when God destroys, when God chooses or rejects, when God allows or disallows, in every way that God reigns, He does so in perfect righteousness. God always acts in perfect harmony with who He is, never in contradiction.

God is the standard of morality.

Many centuries ago, God gave Moses the Law. He began with the Ten Commandments, but went beyond that to offer many guidelines for living out those commandments. We noted earlier that as God gave Moses the Law, He repeatedly inserted the reminder, "I am the Lord." We need to pull that back into focus. Note the opening six verses of Leviticus 18:

> Then the Lord spoke to Moses, saying, "Speak to the children of Israel, and say to them: 'I am the Lord your God. According to the doings of the land of Egypt, where you dwelt, you shall not do; and according to the doings of the land of Canaan, where I am bringing you, you shall not do; nor shall you walk in their ordinances. You shall observe My judgments and keep My ordinances, to walk in them: I am the Lord your God. You shall therefore keep My statutes and My judgments, which if a man does, he shall live by them: I am the Lord.
>
> 'None of you shall approach anyone who is near of kin to him, to uncover his nakedness: I am the Lord.'
>
> *Leviticus 18:1–6*

After sixteen applications of this command, we read this verse: "And you shall not let any of your descendants pass through the fire to Molech, nor shall you profane the name of your God: I am the Lord" (v. 21). Over and over through the following chapters detailing acceptable and unacceptable behavior, God underscores His directions with the same footnote: "I am the Lord" or, "I am the Lord your God."

God Himself is the standard of right and wrong. He did not arbitrarily assign certain behaviors to be morally right and other behaviors to be morally wrong. He gave His people windows into His character. He showed them how His righteousness should be lived out in particular situations they faced.

Whenever God talks to us about what is right or wrong, in some way He is telling us who He is. As the psalmist put it, "Righteous are you, O LORD, and right are your rules" (Psalm 119: 137, ESV).

This has huge implications for us. First, it means the Law is revelatory. It points us to certain realities of God's nature. Through further revelation, of course, we learn that the Law does not tell us everything about who God is—not by a long shot. God is much more than moral standards. In fact, when we try to reduce Him to moral standards, we end up with a barren god, an idolatrous misrepresentation of God. But when we see the commands in the Law as windows into God, and particularly to the righteousness of His person, we understand why the Old Testament saints spoke of the Law with joy and delight.

Let me insert here that God does sometimes direct His people by fiat. Guidance for when and where and how to do specific actions may not be moral directives, but are intended for other purposes. For example, they may provide practical instruction. Other times God gave specific directives that carried symbolic meaning, as in the construction of the tabernacle. These arbitrary decrees, although not specific revelations of God's righteousness, do not violate it.

Seeing God's commands as expressions of who He is also helps us to understand why God took violations of the Law so seriously. When a man or woman said *no* to what God said, they were saying *no* to Him in a very personal way. They were insulting His character. They were saying they knew righteousness better than the One who is altogether righteousness. Doing this would be something like a novice musician—or actually, one who regularly sings off-key—telling a master composer that the pitch, chords, and interpretation indicated in his music are wrong, and singing off-key and out-of-time would make better music. This would not only be an ignorant approach to music, but it would also insult the composer. Imagine the ire of a master musician if such a person gathered a group of likeminded upstarts and they offered a public performance of their "music."

But likeminded fools do this constantly with God. They call good evil and evil good. They conclude that their way of doing life is better than God's way. They promote their ideas through song, literature, and art. Many people think sex, for example, should be a recreational activity between consenting adults with the questions of who, when, and how completely up to them to decide. For sex to be limited to the expression of a lifelong marriage commitment between one man and one woman is seen as restrictive, prudish—not even wise, given the high divorce rate—inhibiting, dangerous to healthy development, and totally unrealistic. People are going to have sex outside of marriage anyway, so teach them to have it responsibly.

God says no sex is allowed outside of a lifelong marriage commitment. We must not think of violations of God's guidelines for sex as simply disobedience to rules. They are violations to something deep in God's nature—insults to His faithfulness, His integrity, His love, and His fierce, enduring commitment in relationship. When people turn sex into selfish gratification, when they strip it of its loyalty and self-sacrificing commitment, they violate the heart of God.

When people steal, they insult the respect and generosity of God. When they lie, they do violence to His honesty and the truth of His being. When they call good people bad and evil people good, they disdain His righteousness. God is in Himself all that is right, true, and good. His laws are expressions of this glorious righteousness. If the world's behavior were transcribed to music, the result would be a horrible dissonance with every instrument tuned to itself and following its own notations—a continual grating of sound on sound. We shouldn't be surprised the Composer is not pleased.

God has stamped His righteousness in our conscience.

Humans are made in God's image. We are "the finite image of the infinite God."[1] Our sense of right and wrong is one way we bear His image—God has stamped His righteousness into our being. In the Fall, the image of God was marred, but not removed.

This is one of the ironies of who we are. We are sinners who regularly violate what God has said, but just as regularly we make moral judgments. We hold others to a standard of morality we don't necessarily follow ourselves. We want to be able to do what we want, get what we want, say what we want, and go where we want. We resent being told we can't do something. In our minds we will bend the rules for ourselves, but we get upset when others do the same thing.

This sense of right and wrong is amazingly strong. We get angry about violations that don't even touch us. When a political or religious leader, for example, cheats on taxes or cheats in marriage or violates children, something stirs deep within us. We want something to be done to make it right—remove the person from office, put him in jail, make him pay.

Sin, then, is not only a violation of who God is, but because we have been made in His image, it is also a violation of who we are. We were not made morally blank. We bear the image of His righteousness in our conscience, and we filter all that we see going on in the world through that moral evaluation. We constantly judge—approve or disapprove—others' actions, words, and motives, and we hold them responsible to do right.

This innate standard, of course, applies to us as well. The judge within also evaluates what we do and say, as well as why we do it. It brings us great pleasure to feel its approval when we are kind to a child, helpful to a needy person, protective of someone in danger, or loyal to a friend at great cost. It heaps shame and disgrace on us when we take advantage of a child or mistreat a person in need.

When we do wrong, we often have some immediate objective in mind—something we want badly enough we are willing to sin to get it. Or we sin because we are in the company of likeminded sinners, and our agreement and mutual enjoyment seem to make it right. Whether it's a group of bullies or gossips having fun at other people's expense, or a crowd of party-goers on a secret tryst, sin can seem so exciting. But when the fun is done, and we are in the silence of solitude or when our sinful behavior comes to the light of public awareness, our conscience rises up like a prosecuting lawyer who will not shut up. It can be merciless. This is one reason that when we live in sin, we hate to be alone and we particularly don't enjoy silence. We don't want to face who we really are.

Paul describes the conscience as God's law "written on the heart," and he says that even people who have not heard the Law of Moses have this inner law. "For when Gentiles, who do not have the law, by nature do what the law requires, they are a law to themselves, even though they do not have the law. They show that the work of the law is written on their hearts, while their conscience also bears witness, and their conflicting thoughts accuse or even excuse them" (Romans 2:14, 15, ESV).

Although this inner lawyer makes us miserable and shows no mercy, it really is God's mercy to have given us such a companion. Our conscience works to keep us from foolish choices and to turn us back to God when we fail. God does not simply want us to feel bad or to stay in condemnation. He wants us to be real, to own up to the truth, to turn from the stupidity of sin and return to Him.

The lines of right and wrong are imbedded forever in the DNA of God. He will never change them to accommodate our desires. The sooner we stop trying to make evil good, the better off we are. We'd call it ridiculous if a man spent his life building an irrigation system where the water had to run uphill, but we are no different when we try to change God's moral standards. It just doesn't work.

Sin distorts our understanding of righteousness.

We've said that God implanted the image of His righteousness on our hearts, that it is amazingly strong and vocal, and that it is particularly quick to pick up on the transgressions of others. Because of our sinfulness, we also work hard at trying to tamper with our sense of right and wrong. We do this to give us loopholes to satisfy our desires, but that isn't the only reason.

We hate being wrong. It is embedded in us. We don't like to hear our own prosecuting lawyer going off about our sins and shortcomings, and we are even more sensitive to the lawyers around us. We hate being judged wrong in the minds of others. So we justify ourselves, hiding wrong behavior behind good motives. Or we explain it in terms that make it seem reasonable—in this case, it was the best thing to do. Or we talk about how hard or impossible it would have been to do otherwise. We blame it on the circumstances, other people, or our health. All these gymnastics are attempts to frame the situation so our wrong behavior looks acceptable. We are trying to change God's eternal righteousness. Crazy, isn't it?

By the way, in the New Testament, the Greek word *dikaioo* is translated either *just* or *righteous*. But there is no verb form of the word righteous in English, so we have only *justify*. What we are trying to do when we justify ourselves is to "righteousify" what we have done. God, of course, has a far better way to "righteousify" us, but that's another subject.

Unfortunately, we actually deceive ourselves with our twisted explanations. We rarely fool one another. We listen to the excuses of others, thinking, *"Yeah, right. You are just plain lazy . . . or greedy or lustful or selfish,"* depending on what they are trying to justify. But when we create fancy rationalizations about our own misbehavior, we come to believe them. We think we are right and that what we have done is morally defensible.

We don't typically think about the futility of our attempts. Futile, because right and wrong are not arbitrary. Trying to shift the lines of right and wrong pits us against God's unchanging character. Trying to recreate Him in our image, we attempt to alter the moral constant of the universe. It's like trying to explain rocks as a liquid. We laugh at the Flat Earth Society, but we are no less laughable when we try to "righteousify" the killing of babies, promiscuous sex, cutting remarks, tax evasion, getting even, shady business deals, twisting the truth, or spreading gossip. It is contrary to reality, and our rationalizing doesn't change anything.

Furthermore, although we've noted that our sense of right and wrong has been implanted in us by the One who is altogether righteous and that we regularly evaluate other people's actions as right or wrong, we must not assume our judgment is always on target. The same sin that skews our thinking badly enough that we think we've pulled one over the All-Righteous One also messes with our judgment of others. When we see someone we don't like doing something right, for example, we easily tuck in a motive that makes the right look wrong. *(Aunt Sally gave me a hug, sure, but she's just trying to make up for always being on my case.)* We project our own selfish motivations on others or suspect them of being stuck-up or snobbish or envious or wanting attention or having a bad attitude. And the more stuck-up or snobbish or envious we are ourselves, the more unreliable is our judgment of others.

While our inner prosecutor has a pretty good sense of what is right or wrong, our sin makes us terrible judges of people, especially when we feel wronged. Because of this wildly inaccurate judgment, we are warned repeatedly not to try to sit as judge; and even more, we are not to carry out sentence against those who wrong us. "Righteous indignation" has motivated more unrighteous action than we can imagine. We simply are not qualified for this business. Only one who is perfectly righteous is in a position to judge rightly and ultimately set things straight.

But our biggest blunders in judgment come when we judge God. Humans do it all the time. Probably the saddest irony of our interaction with a righteous God is that we commonly judge (misjudge) God's ability to run the world in general and our lives in particular. We don't get what we want, and we conclude He doesn't love us. We hit our thumb with a hammer, and we don't understand why God let us have such a bad day. We can't feel God close, and we conclude He is distant or uncaring or isn't saying anything to us. We hit bigger bumps in life—terminal illness, death of a family member, suffering of children, mental illness, unchecked injustice—and we bitterly judge God to be unrighteous for letting such things go on without intervention.

We ask the burning question in many forms: *Why? Why me? Why now? What have I done to deserve this? How can this be right? Why don't You do something? Where is Your power? Don't You care?* When no satisfying answers are forthcoming, we judge God as unrighteous. I wonder how many people in the throes of human suffering have rejected God along these lines of reasoning: "If that's what God is like . . ." Or, "Any God who allows such things to happen . . . " Is any human habit more insidiously anti-God and arrogant than this continual judgment of God's righteousness?

But that is not all. We read the stories under the Old Covenant where God commanded death to transgressors, commanded the annihilation of entire tribes of people, struck down men and women who disobeyed Him, used heathen kings to nearly wipe out His own people, and again we judge Him. But much as we struggle with God's judgments in the past, when we turn to the future we have even bigger problems with God and Hell. The eternal torment of the wicked just doesn't fit our understanding of righteousness. How can a loving God be so harsh? Shuddering at such punishments, we sidle up to the Jesus of the New Covenant who healed the sick, mingled with sinners, and was gentle and uncondemning.

Thus we trade places with God. We put ourselves in the seat as judge, place God in the docket, hold trial, declare the verdict, and pass the sentence. God does a lousy job of running the world. He's made huge blunders in the barbarous past, He has allowed far too much holocaustic behavior and His final solution for the wicked is worse than Hitler's gas chambers. No loving God who is all-powerful would put up with injustice on the scale of world wars or make a world where earthquakes, hurricanes, and tsunamis result in mass destruction. Nor would a loving God allow diseases that cause children to scream in pain, illnesses that turn a healthy athlete into an emaciated corpse, or disorders that waste brilliant minds. Nor would a loving God send my non-Christian friends and neighbors—who aren't terrible people—to Hell. We know. We have a clearer sense of righteousness than God has.

God is righteous in judgment.

Now, I've raised some huge issues. Although I believe that judging God is foolish and arrogant, I want to say that it is not arrogant to have the questions or to wrestle over the answers. Very holy persons have had huge skirmishes here. Job comes to mind, as well as many of the prophets, who often bore the bad news of God's coming judgment not only upon the wicked, but also upon His own people. They delivered the messages, but they struggled with God: "Do you really intend to do this?" Human suffering, divine judgment (past, present, or future), large-scale injustice in the world—these are whopping issues, especially for people of tainted minds. Theologians have held marathon wrestling matches over these doctrinal matters and have judged each other heretics, or sometimes in exhaustion have simply called it a draw.

I do not intend to give a full answer. And I do not intend to, as a matter of faith, not simply as an escape. It seems to me that a full answer is beyond us. If God is who He says He is and we are who He says we are, the way of faith seems much more reasonable. In cases where we don't understand, faith in an all-wise God is more reasonable than the way of unbelief, or the way of forcing facts into an airtight theological system, or the way of demanding answers from God, requiring Him to give account to us.

We are not in a place to stipulate that God must give us satisfactory answers about the righteousness of His acts. Our thinking is not only limited, but clouded with selfishness and sin. God is transcendent. He has to be transcendent to really be God. And if He is so, we must not complain when He doesn't make complete sense to us. This is not the same as saying there is no sense to what He does. Isaiah, who recorded some of the most terrible of God's judgments as well as some of the most glorious revelations of God's mercy, delivered this message from God's heart:

> "For My thoughts are not your thoughts,
> Nor are your ways My ways," says the LORD.
> "For as the heavens are higher than the earth,
> So are My ways higher than your ways,
> And My thoughts than your thoughts."
> *Isaiah 55:8, 9*

If God is transcendent as a person, we should not be surprised that His righteousness transcends our understanding. It seems to me that the first step in trusting God's righteousness is recognizing the inadequacy of our own judgment and the effects of sin upon us. The irony of us holding God (and others) to doing right, even while we regularly fudge on righteousness, ought to give us a healthy humility about judging in general. It should particularly cause us to lay our hands over our mouths when we are tempted to evaluate God and His ways.

In more plain words, when we don't approve of something God has done or said or allowed, we ought first to doubt the rightness of our perspective rather than the righteousness of God. We are limited in time and place and person. Furthermore, we are incredibly selfish. For example, we pray for a sunny day for a picnic or for the traffic to be light or for a short wait in the checkout line with little regard for how these requests might affect people around us. When it rains instead or we get stuck in traffic that causes us to miss an appointment, we get angry at God and rude with people around us. And still we don't get it that our limited perspective and selfish intentions put us in a very poor position to judge right and wrong on the scale of running the world.

Speaking of running the world, God's large-scale judgments of nations and people need to be seen in the bigger picture of history—the story of a great and merciful God over a fallen world, working out His good intentions of revealing Himself to us and redeeming us from our sinfulness, tugging us out of our stubborn unbelief back to faith.

The line of reasoning I have taken—that we ought to trust that God is transcendently righteous—will seem circular or escapist to those who don't know Him (and sometimes to those who know Him but want a better conclusion). My personal peace in this matter rests on God's character. I trust Him. But I do think when we are troubled by something God has done in judgment, we do well to try to see it in the larger picture of His workings. In the bigger view, we often see dimensions of God's mercy that we miss when we zero in on one incident.

We do not have the whole story of every occasion of God's judgment, but the story with the greatest detail is God's judgment on His own people. First the Assyrians wiped out the northern nation of Israel, and then in a series of raids and sieges, the Babylonians destroyed the temple in Jerusalem, carrying off most of the remaining people as captives.

If we stand back and look at the whole story, we don't see a picture of a harsh, trigger-happy God eager to erupt in anger. Just the opposite! God warns His people. He sends prophets who suffer incredibly long with a sin-happy people. He endures insult after insult. Not one of the northern kings followed His ways—all were idol worshipers. The kings of Judah were an up-and-down bunch, but spiraled down toward the end. King Manasseh, as we noted in the last chapter, was an idol-freak, setting up idols and altars to the sun, moon, and foreign gods right in the temple court, even sacrificing his own children on these altars. He oppressed the righteous, and in the words of the chronicler, he "filled Jerusalem" with their blood (2 Kings 21:16). He also promoted sin on a grand scale to the people of Judah.

And yet, although God said such corruption and evil sealed the nation's fate, He delayed judgment for another three generations. He used a heathen king to strike King Manasseh personally. Manasseh was taken to Babylon and there in a prison cell, he broke down, repented of his sins, and prayed for forgiveness. God forgave him and even restored him to his throne in Jerusalem!

Our God is a forgiving God, a longsuffering God, a God who delays the deserved punishment of sinners far beyond what humans—even judicious ones—would. If that were not enough, in Manasseh's personal story and in the larger Jewish history we see that God's judgment was filled with mercy and redemption. Over and over God's judgment has been shown to bring about repentance and restoration rather than annihilation.

Even the curse God placed on the earth with the coming of sin was not intended simply to make life difficult for us, but to show us the true nature of sin, to make the way of transgression hard, and to turn us from our sin. God was not acting peevishly when He cursed the earth; it was a huge act of mercy. What kind of world would this be if sin had no consequences, if fallen humans lived with no losses, calamity, or hardship to wake us up to our condition and turn us to our Redeemer?

But there is a limit. When individuals and nations pass the point of redemption, God brings the true end of their ways upon them. This is righteous. The end of sin is death. It cannot be otherwise, because there is simply no ongoing life apart from God. We may resist God for a time, persist in our own ways for years, but we cannot go on in this attempt to twist the laws of the universe forever. As one writer said so succinctly, "There are only two kinds of people in the end: those who say to God, 'Thy will be done,' and those to whom God says, in the end, '*Thy* will be done.'"[2]

God's judgment, whether on the grand scale of the Flood or a smaller scale such as the destruction of Sodom and Gomorrah, is always righteous. The coming destruction of the world—the "day of the Lord" foretold by many prophets—will be righteous. Though it holds untold terror for the wicked, because it is a work of God, it will be a glorious work. God will fulfill His good intention for a good world. He will uphold His commitment to the redeemed of all ages—His tender, unfailing love and care for them in a wicked world—by setting the world right.

In judgment, God will be all that God is—good and loving and merciful and altogether righteous. All God's people wait and hope for this great and final work of setting everything right, putting down everything wrong, and ushering in the age where righteousness is the order of everything and the character of everyone. All creation groans for this day.

> Let the field be joyful, and all that is in it.
> Then all the trees of the woods will rejoice
> before the Lord.
> For He is coming, for He is coming to judge the earth.
> He shall judge the world with righteousness,
> And the peoples with His truth.
> *Psalm 96:12, 13*

When God's judgment is revealed for what it is, it will be a righteous work to be celebrated. Not one will be able to point a finger at God and say it was not right. This is the stance of faith on which our unanswered questions must rest. We don't have the final word about who spends eternity with God and who does not or how either group will be treated. It is not given to us to decide where our helpful but unbelieving neighbor will spend eternity—or the heathen who have never heard the Gospel, or Hitler, or Mother Teresa. That is God's work. And the same God who planned the glorious surprises of eternity for the redeemed is the Sovereign Judge over eternal punishment. He is not a different God, and everything He does is right, right, right.

God's righteousness has different levels.

It is easy to think of righteousness as a relatively simple matter. *There's right and there's wrong, and that's that.* Unfortunately, we often operate that way, even as believers. But if we are willing to draw near to the great God of the whole Bible, we begin to see a righteousness that leaves our minds spinning. (We might have expected this, knowing Him!)

We believe that God's revelation to us has been progressive. As the writer to the early Hebrew believers put it, "God, who at various times and in various ways spoke in time past to the fathers by the prophets, has in these last days spoken to us by His Son, whom He has appointed heir of all things, through whom also He made the worlds; who being the brightness of His glory and the express image of His person, and upholding all things by the word of His power, when He had by Himself purged our sins, sat down at the right hand of the Majesty on high" (Hebrews 1:1–3). Like an unfolding story in which we learn to know the characters little by little by observing their words and actions, we learn to know God through the grand story of the ages. We learn first that He is the Creator—the originator of all things. In this He also shows that He is both all-powerful and good. He can make whatever He wants with just a spoken command, and what He makes He pronounces very good. We get windows into His love, His righteousness, His mercy, and His sovereignty in the stories of the Fall, Cain and Abel, Noah, the Flood, the choosing of Abraham, the birth of Isaac, Jacob's conniving, Jacob's sons, their sojourn in Egypt, and then the Hebrews' deliverance from Egypt and extended journey to Canaan.

God's righteousness is alive and working in all these parts of the big story. But when the Israelites stopped at Mt. Sinai, a whole chapter of this grand story is devoted to a special revelation of His righteousness. It came in the form of the Law. We've already noted that as God told His people how to behave, He was revealing to them His righteousness.

The revelation of God's righteousness via the Law focuses on what we might think of as the righteousness of equity. It required just scales in business, boundary lines in possessions and ownership, faithfulness to one's word in relationships, and just punishment in legal and civil affairs. In law, equity is epitomized by the *lex taliones*: eye for eye, tooth for tooth, life for life. As many have pointed out, this equity in punishment was not intended as a demand that must always be met, but a limitation against our sinful tendency to revenge beyond what is just. Somebody takes out a tooth, and we want to take out his whole face.

Furthermore, even the *lex taliones* was not a harsh, unbending requirement. It took into account such matters as intent and circumstances. If a man injured another by accident, his wrongdoing was not treated the same as a premeditated crime. If a man stole under the duress of hunger, the punishment was softened accordingly.

The laws of equity are righteous, rooted firmly in the character of God. We might see them as a baseline righteousness, intended to mark out the line between fair and foul, right and wrong, with precision. A one-pound weight on one side of the scales measures out one pound of goods on the other. To alter the weight in order to sell three-fourths of a pound of goods for the price of a pound of goods is to cross the line from right to wrong. The law immediately cries "Foul!" when we cross that line.

In our fallenness we seem to be fixated on finding ways to alter the line without getting caught. We are prone to live along the line, reaching across without stepping across. And sometimes the more the line is emphasized by our authorities, the more we look for ways to get around it.

Our inner lawyer, by the way, is aligned with this righteousness of equity. Though we get a perverse sense of satisfaction out of trying to move it around for ourselves, we are quick to point out when others step across, especially when they do so in violation of our territory.

Fortunately, equity is not all there is to God's righteousness, or we would be toast. If our sin against Him were met with immediate and equitable justice, we would no longer exist. The just punishment for departing from God, setting up ourselves as our own determiners of right and wrong, and walking according to our own ways is death. There is no life possible apart from God. But God is more than the standard of right and wrong, and more than the Judge of the universe. Much more!

When we move beyond baseline righteousness, we find levels of righteousness far above equity. Beyond just scales in business is the righteousness of generosity. Beyond respect for property lines we can experience neighborly kindness and assistance. Helping our friends, assisting those in need, giving to the poor, caring for the weak, protecting the handicapped—these levels of righteousness reach far beyond the border of right and wrong. The big word for righteousness above the law is *love*. Love offers us an immense and free range of righteous living—words, actions, attitudes—open to us every day.

God is this kind of God. This is His character. He continually operates in generosity, thoughtfulness, kindness, and helpfulness, especially toward His people. This is why we pray. We are continually in need, and He is continually our generous provider, giver, and protector far beyond what we "earn" or deserve by any just measure.

Under the Old Covenant, it seems the revelation of God's righteousness was especially focused on these two levels of His righteousness. He wanted His people to understand baseline righteousness, knowing the line between right and wrong, clean and unclean, holy and profane. In that clear light, He also wanted them to learn the righteousness of generosity, kindness, and helpfulness.

We cannot understand generosity if we do not know equity. We do not realize the wonderful blessing of giving if we do not first learn to respect property lines. Built into the civil laws that forbade stealing, lying, oppression, and killing were also laws that marked out how generosity and helpfulness were to be lived out. The commands that called for tithing and thank offerings, the sabbatical years, the release of debtors, and the year of Jubilee were intended to encourage generosity and goodwill beyond simple equity.

But this is not all. The righteousness of God's love is not limited to generosity toward His people. God extends His love even to His enemies. We see reflections of this kind of love in the Old Covenant, though it was not fully revealed until Jesus came. "God so loved the world that He gave His only begotten Son," John wrote in that golden text of the Bible. Paul clarified it even further, "For scarcely for a righteous man will one die; yet perhaps for a good man someone would even dare to die. But God demonstrates His own love toward us, in that while we were still sinners, Christ died for us" (Romans 5:7, 8). God is that kind of God—willing to extend His love to sinners, to self-serving rebels, to those who oppose Him, resist Him, fight against Him, and finally nail Him to a Roman cross.

Under the New Covenant, God asks all those who believe in His Son to demonstrate the same kind of love to their enemies. He tells us not to take an eye for an eye, not to retaliate with force against those who would harm us, not to demand justice for wrongs against us (even though these would be our "rights"), but to leave all redress to Him. Our only "weapon" in a sinful world is love. We are called to follow Jesus in the way of love, to display, as it were, this cruciform love of God that was willing to suffer and die to redeem sinners.

Following Jesus' way, we are called to meet hatred with love, cursing with blessing, violence with kindness, and injustice with forgiveness. This righteousness far exceeds the law of equity and surpasses even generosity. Even sinners can demonstrate generosity toward friends, but kindness and goodwill toward enemies is a righteousness rooted in God's heart.

We must not think this is an altogether different righteousness or a different God from the God of the Old Covenant. The righteousness of love is above the laws of equity, but not opposed to them. Justice is still with us in mercy. This reality cuts a number of ways. First, Jesus explained that the love and forgiveness we extend to those who sin against us is rooted firmly in the love and forgiveness God has extended to us. We forgive "as we have been forgiven," which means over and over, generously and freely. The mercy we have received calls us, even by the law of equity, to show the same kind of mercy to others. In other words, it is only right and just that people who have been so lavishly loved and forgiven offer the same to others.

Furthermore, the mercy and kindness shown to us through Jesus heighten the stakes of justice. If spurning the laws of God's righteousness deserves punishment, what kind of punishment is deserved for spurning God's love in Jesus! This warning is repeated several times in the letter to the Hebrews. These Jewish believers knew the Law of Moses very well and they knew the consequences for violating it. The writer urges them to recognize that the greater revelation calls for more careful attention. If the word of God in the Law was important, how much more the living Word of God in the person of Jesus! If disregard for the Sabbath deserved punishment, how much more does disregard for the Lord of the Sabbath!

"Anyone who has rejected Moses' law dies without mercy on the testimony of two or three witnesses. Of how much worse punishment, do you suppose, will he be thought worthy who has trampled the Son of God underfoot, counted the blood of the covenant by which he was sanctified a common thing, and insulted the Spirit of grace?" (Hebrews 10:28, 29). Thus while the righteousness of love is above the righteousness of just punishment, it is not an opposite, neither is it a separate or foreign kind of righteousness. These levels of righteousness operate in perfect harmony in the same God.

"The law was given through Moses, but grace and truth came through Jesus Christ" (John 1:17). The greater, deeper, richer experiences of God's grace in Jesus heighten the sin of spurning it. Thus God's mercy—the higher level of righteousness—does not abandon God's justice at the baseline. All the righteousness of God is right. In showing us higher levels of righteousness, Jesus made it clear He was not doing away with the lower levels. He was simply calling us to follow Him in demonstrating the Father's love and grace to a broken world, leaving the redress up to the Father. Even as the Father is unparalleled in His demonstration of grace, He is also unparalleled in His execution of justice. Summing up the consistency of God's righteousness and mercy, Tozer says:

> All of God's acts are consistent with all of His attributes. . . . The familiar picture of God as often torn between His justice and His mercy is altogether false to the facts. To think of God as inclining first toward one and then toward another of His attributes is to imagine a God who is unsure of Himself, frustrated and emotionally unstable, which of course is to say that the one of whom we are thinking is not the true God at all but a weak, mental reflection of Him badly out of focus.[3]

The God of the Old Covenant is not a different God than the Jesus of the New Covenant. The Lion is also a Lamb, and the Lamb is also a Lion. He who runs the world laid down His life for it. He who laid down His life for the world will set the whole world to right in the end—perfectly and forever.

WALKING WITH GOD

1. The journey into God's righteousness has surprising twists. Ponder these thoughts:

    a. God is thoroughly righteous forever. He loves righteousness and hates sin.

    b. God had placed the imprint of His righteousness on our moral reasoning, which we call conscience. It acts as an "inner light," and it is quick to pass moral judgment on others and even on God.

    c. Sin continually clouds our moral reasoning, creating pathetic ironies as we justify ourselves, condemn others, live in fear of condemnation, and find ourselves as God's people sometimes rightly rebuked by sinners.

    d. God is far too often judged as unrighteous by human upstarts.

    e. This righteous God has gone to incredible lengths to reconcile unrighteous humans to Himself.

2. Think of times you have thought ill of God or His ways. What acts of God in history trouble you most? In what situations in your own life have you been tempted to charge God with unrighteousness?

3. The biblical writers, particularly the psalmists and the prophets, reflect struggles with God's righteousness. They cry out when it seems to them God has not acted in righteousness. In these cries, they are very honest, and yet they return to affirm God's righteousness.

    a. Struggles with God's righteousness include the following:

        i. Abraham, Genesis 18:16–33, see especially verse 25.
        ii. Job, see especially chapters 9 and 10.
        iii. Habakkuk (already studied in chapter 5, but see 1:12 and following verses).
        iv. Asaph, Psalm 73.

b. Affirmations of God's righteousness:

   i. "Full of splendor and majesty is his work, and his righteousness endures forever. . . . The works of his hands are faithful and just" (Psalm 111:3, 7, ESV).

   ii. "Therefore all Your precepts concerning all things I consider to be right" (Psalm 119:128).

   iii. "O Lord God of Israel, You are righteous"! (Ezra 9:15, where Ezra is overwhelmed with shame for the sins of the returned exiles.)

4. If God is always righteous and we face situations where He appears not to be so, what are our options for finding a different perspective?

5. Paul adamantly declares God's righteousness in the forgiveness of sins through Jesus (see Romans 3:24–26). In your own words, tell how you understand God to be righteous in forgiving sinners.

6. Make a list of events from the Old Testament where you see God's righteousness.

7. Jesus was often in conflict with the religious rulers over matters of righteousness. They often accused Him of wrongdoing when He was doing good. At one point, He said to them, "Do not judge according to appearance, but judge with righteous judgment" (John 7:24). Probably nowhere in the New Testament is the contrast between His view of righteousness and theirs so clearly stated as in His denunciation of the Pharisees in Matthew 23. These are potent words. You may wish to meditate on them and begin a list of observations about God's righteousness, or you might study this passage to contrast man's view of righteousness with God's view.

Notes

1. Daniel Kauffman, *Doctrines of the Bible* (Scottdale, PA: Herald Press, 1928), 83.

2. C. S. Lewis, *The Best of C. S. Lewis* (Grand Rapids: Baker Book House, 1969), 156.

3. A. W. Tozer, *The Knowledge of the Holy* (New York: Harper & Row Publishers, 1961), 85.

GOD IS SOVEREIGN

The Most High rules in the kingdom of men,
and gives it to whomever He chooses. . . .
All the inhabitants of the earth are reputed as nothing;
He does according to His will in the army of heaven
And among the inhabitants of the earth.
No one can restrain His hand
Or say to Him, "What have You done?"

DANIEL 4:25, 35

God is sovereign. Whooo boy! We are in over our heads here even as we take our first step into this deep. God rules the world. We believe He accomplishes His good purposes in (and even through) the affairs of wicked men and the failures of His own people. Opponents make no progress against Him—He uses their very efforts to accomplish His own intentions. He throws down the mighty. He lifts up the fallen. He saves. He destroys. Much of what is considered great in human history is trivial in His sight, and many who are considered nobodies He has used to do the impossible.

Well, that's what we are up against. As your guide into acquaintance with this God, I feel like I'm barely out of the crawling stage. When I resort to babbling in this chapter, I ask you to smile at my immaturity and try to see on my face and hear from my lips an infant's delighted shrieks as he gazes at the Majesty on high!

As sovereign, God does as He pleases.

God's ability to run the world is a theological pillar. It is a pillar we trust when all else is crumbling around us. But we don't see the glory of the sovereign God just by trying to measure the pillar—its base, its breadth, its height, its consistency. Sigh of relief! We would wear out a million shovels trying to dig to the roots of this pillar. We break our flimsy hammers (and our minds) trying to analyze a chip of God's sovereignty.

I do not mean that the systematic theologies are no good. I only mean they attempt to chart territory beyond where humans have been. And arguably they are not the best route to experiencing His Sovereignty, necessary as they truly are.

One way to gain insight into God's sovereignty is to observe Him at work through the ages. Seeing God rule the world from this vantage point inspires both immeasurable terror and unspeakable comfort.

Let's start at the beginning when God made the universe. Into the expanse of nothingness, He sent spinning galaxies—novas, supernovas, black holes, matter and antimatter, giant stars, white dwarfs, suns with their planets, comets, rings of fire, and clouds of dust. Even with the most powerful telescopes, we are only now beginning to see the vastness and wonder of the heavens God spoke into existence.

He made the earth, teeming with life. Aquatic life—all kinds of fish (in fresh water and salt), thousands of varieties of crustaceans, magnificent coral reefs, and water habitats that vary from seas to swamps to rivers to lakes, from tropical to arctic. Forests—trees and bushes bearing nuts and fruits, offering a home to everything from birds to climbing animals to bugs and cicadas and spiders. Earthy habitats of grass and moss and rotting vegetation for untold numbers of creeping, crawling, slithering things as well as for animals that burrow. He made mountains and deserts and plains and tropics and coastal seaboards, each with its unique cast of animals and birds and insects and plant life, eating, dying, and reproducing after their kind. Systems—weather patterns, fronts, storms, entire climates, warming and cooling patterns, *El Niño,* northern lights, chinooks . . .

God made it all. And according to the Scriptures, God is "upholding all things by the word of His power" (Hebrews 1:3). He's the One who set it all in motion, and He's the One who keeps it all going. The life and vitality and motion and "laws" of the world (everything from magnetism to gravity to aerodynamics to climates to reproduction) are continually ordered along by God's sovereign word.

In everything He made, God is working out His intentions. And as we noticed when we explored God's faithfulness, we continually rely on His ordered world—gravity is always pulling matter together in a constant force, we rely on electricity to be consistent from day to day, we make weather forecasts because we depend on the laws of moisture and temperature and fronts to remain constant. What we are saying now is that God is in all this at all times—He not only made it but He also runs it to accomplish His will. God is sovereign over all that He made.

Elihu, the young man who held his tongue until Job's friends exhausted their criticism, gave a strong defense of God. Though we've never figured out for sure if Elihu was part of Job's troubles or the start of Job's restoration, he was soundly on target in his argument that God runs the world.

> God's voice thunders in marvelous ways;
>   he does great things beyond our understanding.
> He says to the snow, 'Fall on the earth,'
>   and to the rain shower, 'Be a mighty downpour.'
> So that all men he has made may know his work,
>   he stops every man from his labor.
> The animals take cover;
>   they remain in their dens.
> The tempest comes out from its chamber,
>   the cold from the driving winds.
> The breath of God produces ice,
>   and the broad waters become frozen.
> He loads the clouds with moisture;
>   he scatters his lightning through them.
> At his direction they swirl around
>   over the face of the whole earth

to do whatever he commands them.
He brings the clouds to punish men,
or to water his earth and show his love.
Job 37:5–13, NIV

God's works are not seen just in the world of nature, but as Nebuchadnezzar observed, God has His way in the "kingdoms of men" as well. He chose Abraham, Isaac, and Jacob from among all the people of the earth (others at that time were God-fearing, too, such as Melchizedek). He called their descendants His "chosen people." He made them into a nation, brought them out of Egypt, and gave them a homeland. He watched over them through centuries of ups and downs, but finally, in their disobedience, He decimated the nation—down to the foundation stones of their sacred temple—and gave them into the hands of foreigners.

Even in their captivity, He did things only God could do. Some of the most impossible stories in the Bible come out of that era—Daniel's interpretation of dreams, his deliverance from lions, his three friends rescued untouched from a blazing furnace, Esther laying her life on the line, Mordecai rescuing the king's life and in turn being honored by his worst enemy.

Then came the restoration of a remnant to their homeland, and we read about Ezra's inspiring love for the Scriptures and Nehemiah's courageous leadership. God was over all those people all through those centuries, working out His good purposes.

God's rule extends beyond His own people. His rule is over all the people of the earth. At the same time He is calling Abram, He sees Sodom's wickedness. While He makes His people into a nation, He is fully aware of the greed and pride of the trading cities along the Mediterranean coast. He monitors the moral slide of the Hittite nations in Canaan. Even as He allows nations to punish His own people, He notices when the Edomites mock the Israelites, and warns them about their pride. Even as He sees the rise of the Assyrians to the north, He speaks of the future Babylonian Empire, of the Medo-Persians who will destroy the Babylonians, and of the Greeks led by a world conqueror. He sees not only the evil in these nations, but also the good. He knows that sending Jonah to Nineveh will result in repentance. He knows that the Syrian army captain, Naaman, and the proud and mighty Nebuchadnezzar will humble themselves and become worshipers of Jehovah.

While this great God is seeing all this in clear detail, He is running things, setting up and throwing down, holding rulers and peoples accountable for their actions, and moving in these events of men and nations to set the stage for sending His Son into the world. And "when the fullness of the time had come, God sent forth His Son, born of a woman, born under the law, to redeem those who were under the law, that we might receive the adoption as sons" (Galatians 4:4, 5). God really does run the world.

God delegated dominion of the earth to humans.

A focus on God's sovereignty in nature and nations can be misleading. God truly is over everything, working out His great intentions. But God is also near and personal and interactive with us. If we had only the great, transcendent view of His sovereignty, we might conclude that such a Sovereign will do as He pleases, and our actions, choices, plans, and work is meaningless. But this would be a caricature of God. He certainly could run the world without us and completely in spite of us, but He has chosen an interactive relationship with us. This is both a puzzle and a wonder, but like God's sovereign reign far above us, this rulership "with us" also runs through all the pages of the world's story.

We need to go back to the beginning again and view it from this vantage point. God commissioned Adam and Eve to "be fruitful and multiply; fill the earth and subdue it; have dominion over the fish of the sea, over the birds of the air, and over every living thing that moves on the earth" (Genesis 1:28). God delegated the rulership of the earth to humans. This does not mean absolute sovereignty, of course, for we have limitations in both ability and morality (though immorality at that point had not yet been disastrously explored). Within the limitations of ability, Adam and Eve had the run of the earth. They could do anything they pleased to exercise dominion over the land, the animals, and the earth's resources because anything they pleased at that time was thoroughly good. They had freedom within limitations, choice within boundaries. But the freedom was large, the choices wide. As coworkers with God, they had millions of wide-open possibilities to explore, develop, cultivate, invent, make, and build.

This is at least in part what it means to be made in God's image. We are not equals with Him, but creatures with qualities in finite form that God holds in infinity. Even as God is sovereign, we, too, were wired to "run things," to bring order to our surroundings, to plant and harvest, to build and arrange. Like God, we do this not only for functionality, but for beauty and personal delight, and maybe even more significantly, for personal expression. We look at a lady's kitchen, for example, and say, "That is so Barbara!" We do this sort of God-like work because we were made in His image.

Humans have usurped the throne.

As the only absolute sovereign, God has delegated the rule of the earth to humans. But we've got a problem, one that has made a huge mess. We are fallen from our original goodness. We fell exactly because we were made to be creatures of choice. One of the paths open to us led directly to the forbidden fruit, and ever since Eve bit into it, we seem intent on tasting it yet again, satisfying our desires in our own ways rather than God's ways, brewing new concoctions of disobedience.

Yes, disobedience is intoxicating. It has drugged our minds, slurred our speech, dulled our senses, and made us hallucinate badly. Paul describes the unredeemed as living "in the futility of their mind, having their understanding darkened, being alienated from the life of God, because of the ignorance that is in them, because of the blindness of their heart; who, being past feeling, have given themselves over to lewdness, to work all uncleanness with greediness" (Ephesians 4:17–19). Coming back to God is like recovering from the stupor of an addiction.

But this is us. Having been given the rulership of the earth under the sovereignty of a wise and good God, we wanted absolute rulership, at least in our own territory. We coveted the throne of our lives. Instead of working in loving cooperation with God, carrying out our responsibilities and exploring our opportunities within His good intentions, we wanted full rights to choose our own ways. Once sin had settled in, the delusion that our ways were better pervaded our thinking like a heavy fog. We became lost in ourselves and slaves to sin.

What looked like freedom was actually bondage. What looked like taking the throne of our lives put us behind bars. Our rebellion—laying claim to sovereignty—did not threaten God's throne in the least, any more than an infant's balled fists or insistent squalls threaten its father as he cradles it. This picture of a tender father and squalling infant, although it may somewhat capture the difference in moods between God and His wayward children, does not come close to capturing the difference in sovereignty. The gap between father and child is a small gap between fellow mortals, while the difference between the sovereign God and self-governing miscreants is the vastness between the finite and the infinite. No, the rebellion was not a threat to God, but it did immeasurable harm to us.

God still honors human choice.

Although the plunge into sin twisted our understanding of freedom and turned our habits of choice into exercises in self-destruction, God still honors human choice. Even as He called to Adam and Eve in the Garden after their disobedience, He has continued to call us. His call has become clearer and more insistent with the unfolding revelation of Himself. God called people to Himself through the Law, through the prophets, through visions and dreams, through His mighty works, through the record of those works in the Scriptures, and finally through His Son. His call is a call of repentance—*turn in sorrow from trying to run your own lives*—and it is a call to return to loving relationship with the Father. As He calls, God respects the wonderful gift we have of choosing to respond to Him and at the same time allows us the terrible option of refusing. Some return to Him. Many do not.

What we are noting here, however, is that we have the two dimensions to the way God runs the world. We have His sovereignty over everything and everyone. We also have, within that sovereignty, God allowing men and women to make personal choices. He bears upon them through the circumstances of life. He works within them by His Spirit. But He does not snuff out human choice or run roughshod over it. He is "not willing that any should perish" (2 Peter 3:9), but He honors the power of our choice to submit to His will or to resist His will, even to our own destruction.

This is both respectful of us and awful in its implications. It accounts for much of the contradictory way we think about our choices. On the one hand, we insist on the freedom to choose. From small choices of what to eat and what to wear to the larger choices of career and life companion, we resist the thought of choices being made for us. We'd feel used and less than human if everything in life were simply the ordering of a sovereign authority. Determinism—even a divine determinism—is a depressing view of life, not an energizing one.

But on the other hand, we lament when human choices are left unchecked, particularly when they are destructive. We hear this from the lips of unbelievers as a criticism about God—if He is God, why doesn't He step in and stop genocide, rescue those who are being used in the sex trade, and protect children from abusive parents? Even while they say this, they insist on the right to run their own lives, have their own views, practice their own sins, and make their own judgments. They want God to limit the freedom of other sinners, while allowing them to practice their own sins—as if there were harmless sins.

All this is not to say that life is all up to us or that our freedom to choose is all it appears to be or that God is as passive as He sometimes appears. It is rather to acknowledge God's sovereignty and the freedom of human choice working simultaneously (though not equally) through life's events with neither obliterating the other.

Thus in election we see God's sovereignty working both "in spite of" and "because of." God chose Abraham, a man who spoke half-truths. "She is my sister" was partly true, but he said it to deceive men about Sarah's status as his wife. Isaac told an outright lie—Rebekah was not his sister. Jacob was an accomplished deceiver, lying not to strangers, but to his own father. His sons—the fathers of God's chosen people—brought the lying home to Jacob, deceiving him about his favorite son.

God chose these people in spite of their faults. In the words of Moses to the Israelites, "The LORD did not set His love on you nor choose you because you were more in number than any other people, for you were the least of all peoples; but because the LORD loves you, and because He would keep the oath which He swore to your fathers, the LORD has brought you out with a mighty hand, and redeemed you from the house of bondage, from the hand of Pharaoh king of Egypt. Therefore know that the LORD your God, He is God" (Deuteronomy 7:–9). Here the "because" rests clearly in God's sovereign (and loving) heart.

But in the same stories, we observe God acting upon the responses of people. In one of the most profound verses of the Old Testament, we read, "[Abram] believed in the LORD, and He accounted it to him for righteousness" (Genesis 15:6). Over and over we find the sovereign God honoring those who honor Him, and we also find God requiring an account from those who disregard Him. When His people worshiped Him, called upon Him, and followed His ways, He showered them with blessings of provision, protection, and deliverance. And when they turned to follow other gods and pursue their own ways, He brought hardship and ruin to show them their folly and turn them back to Him. God's workings are clearly not arbitrary or unilateral—the "because" of His doings interacts with the responses of His people.

Much has been the wrangling over the sovereignty of God in our salvation. Does salvation and damnation of individuals depend on God's sovereign choice alone or does it depend on man's response to God's call? We find theologians shouting at each other from the opposite horns of this dilemma. The Scriptures address this question from various vantage points, and we must honor all God says here without making one of His statements obliterate another one. For example, God said to Moses, "I will be gracious to whom I will be gracious, and I will have compassion on whom I will have compassion" (Exodus 33:19). And Jesus said, "No one can come to Me unless the Father who sent Me draws him" (John 6:44).

Here we observe God's sovereign hand and heart in salvation. On the other hand, God consistently calls for human responses and holds us accountable for how we respond. "I call heaven and earth as witnesses today against you, that I have set before you life and death, blessing and cursing; therefore choose life, that both you and your descendants may live; that you may love the LORD your God, that you may obey His voice, and that you may cling to Him, for He is your life and the length of your days" (Deuteronomy 30:19, 20).

Jesus, in a remarkable statement about the responses to His message, said,

> Woe to you, Chorazin! Woe to you, Bethsaida! For if the mighty works which were done in you had been done in Tyre and Sidon, they would have repented long ago in sackcloth and ashes. But I say to you, it will be more tolerable for Tyre and Sidon in the day of judgment than for you. And you, Capernaum, who are exalted to heaven, will be brought down to Hades; for if the mighty works which were done in you had been done in Sodom, it would have remained until this day. But I say to you that it shall be more tolerable for the land of Sodom in the day of judgment than for you".
>
> *Matthew 11:21–24*

Clearly Jesus places the responsibility to repent and be saved upon those who heard His message and saw His miracles. Even more astounding, He says others would have responded differently, and consequently their condition on the day of judgment would have been different! Salvation requires a voluntary response for which we are held accountable and upon which God acts.

God is sovereign in election, yes, and at the same time God has given humans both the capacity and the responsibility to choose. We must hold these two truths simultaneously without using one to knock out the other. As Norman Geisler summarizes: "God's predestination and human free choice are a mystery, but not a contradiction. They go beyond reason, but not against reason. That is, they are not incongruous, but neither can we see exactly how they are complementary. We apprehend each as true, but we do not comprehend how both are true."[1]

In an attempt to bring together the truth of God's election and man's free will, Randy Alcorn says:

> I certainly believe in man's free will, but also believe it has clear limits. Some go to one extreme and think of us as automatons with no true freedom to choose, mechanical men wandering the deck of a ship, some destined to clean the decks, some stuck in the engine rooms, some to steal purses. They think free will is an illusion. All is fate or sovereign design. They cite Romans' references to people who are "vessels of wrath created for destruction," but there are many other passages that invite people to come and choose and drink freely of the water of life.
>
> Others err, though, in envisioning us as fully free to determine the course of our lives, captains of the ship, capable of doing whatever we wish, taking the ship to any harbor and destiny, without fear of the ship sinking or our plans being ultimately thwarted. In some cases, they see Him as a deistic God who got it all started then abandoned ship, with no real interest or control. We're on our own, and we're "captains of our fate."
>
> A more biblical analogy, I think, is that we have true freedom to walk the ship, to choose when and where to eat, whether or not we befriend other passengers. We can do good or evil. We can stay on the ship or even jump overboard. But we do not have control over exactly where the ship is going, the sway of the sea, the weather—sunshine or storms—and whether we ultimately live or die.[2]

The journey into God's sovereignty is perhaps the most unknowing of all the paths in our walk with God. Our minds simply cannot stretch into such limitlessness. But the great story of all God's workings through the centuries demonstrates His ability to run the universe, rule the world, and have His way in the lives of all people even while allowing us freedom to make choices.

If we make this solely an intellectual journey, we are apt to run down one pathway or another (a five-point-ism or counter-ism) and look for evidence or logic to tackle other intellectuals. It is not wrong to have ideas or offer explanations at the level we understand. But even in our best explanations, if we do not lay our hands over our mouths in humility and go on our knees in adoration, we are apt to create more heat than light, as the saying goes. Intellectual arrogance, even at a high level of understanding, is worse than the heartfelt wonder of a person who simply trusts God's sovereignty without full explanation.

Satan usurped the throne of earth.

We haven't yet talked about the third player in the rulership of the earth. We don't know much about the story of his fallout with God, but according to Jesus, Satan "fell from heaven" (see Luke 10:18). We see him first in the Garden of Eden in the form of a snake, talking to Eve, fouling her pure mind, and ultimately trying to ruin God's good work. We see him through the story of God's redemptive work, goading men and women toward ruinous decisions, driving whole cultures madly down paths of sensuality and destruction. In the stories of Job and other saints, Satan roams the earth concocting devilish mischief, accusing the righteous, defacing human existence with pain and suffering, and enjoying every opportunity to befuddle their minds and destroy their happiness. Jesus rightly named him a murderer and a liar from the beginning (John 8:44).

But Satan is more than a spoiler. He, too, desires rulership, and he exercises governance—a usurped governance—over the world system. We do not know all he does or how he does it, but he is called the "god of this world" (2 Corinthians 4:4, ESV), and he and his fallen cohorts are referred to as "principalities, . . . powers, . . . rulers of the darkness of this age, . . . spiritual hosts of wickedness in the heavenly places" (Ephesians 6:12). Those who persist in their own rebellion against God are inadvertently Satan's slaves, members of the resistance movement against God's kingdom, and destined to share in his ultimate destruction.

Because we do not know much about Satan's rule, we do best not to speculate about its actual workings. Enough for us to know that our own rebellion against God is a small-town operation in comparison to his, and furthermore, that if God is capable of snuffing out the resistance of multitudes of twisted angels and turning their efforts against Himself to accomplish their own destruction and actually carry forward His redemptive purposes, our own resistance to Him is pathetically short-sighted. We should flee back to the good Sovereign of the universe while mercy is offered.

God reigns.

Jesus came proclaiming the kingdom of God. As the Son of God, He knows His Father intimately, understands His kind intentions for humans, is fully acquainted with both our peril and our foolishness, and in coming to earth was committed to breaking the enemy's power and setting the stage to restore God's reign on the earth.

During His time among us, Jesus both proclaimed and demonstrated the kingdom of God. Wherever He went, He announced that the kingdom "is at hand." He spoke of His own decisions and work as "doing the will of the Father." Doing the Father's will is demonstrating His reign, bringing in His kingdom. As Jesus lived out the Father's will, He showed us that humans are intended to live and breathe and do and love the Father's will.

Jesus also demonstrated it is both good and possible to live out the kingdom of God in a fallen world. Because of Jesus, we cannot say that living out God's will is impractical in our world. It may not be easy and it may ruffle feathers, especially among the self-righteous, but it is the best way to live. The Father's will in a fallen world is to love the unlovely, care for the downtrodden and destitute, forgive the penitent, comfort the brokenhearted, warn the proud and unbelieving, make known the Father, and commit to His good intentions for a redeemed humanity in a renewed world.

Jesus also demonstrated the kingdom of God by throwing back the works of Satan. He healed those who were crippled, blinded, and diseased by the enemy. He cast out demons from those who were oppressed and bound in spiritual chains. He sent out seventy of His disciples, telling them to declare to everyone that "the kingdom of

God has come near to you"! (Luke 10:9) and giving them "authority to trample on serpents and scorpions, and over all the power of the enemy" (v. 19). From the context, we assume "serpents and scorpions" refers to the diseases and demons they were to drive out by His authority. By this Jesus demonstrated that although wickedness is rampant, it is not the final word. The world is not spinning out of control. It has been invaded by the God of the universe who has vowed to set it right, and to do so in a way that reveals His redemptive power. As sovereign, He could wipe out evil with one flick of His eyelashes, but He has set out to make a statement, to demonstrate that He not only reigns, but that He redeems from evil.

The resurrection of Jesus is the most powerful demonstration of God's sovereign, redemptive power. The mystery here stretches beyond our full comprehension, but we see God's power and authority and love and mercy and righteousness coming together in the mind-boggling crucifixion and resurrection of Jesus. He allowed evil men to kill Him, showing love and mercy rather than just and immediate retribution. He allowed the powers of evil to do their worst with His human form, nailing it through flesh and sinew to the cross. The Author of life entered death itself! And as the Spirit of the sovereign God entered again into His broken, dead body, He not only came to life, but He tore death, disease, and decay from the power of the enemy. He broke the back of the resistance movement.

In this event we see men choosing to resist God—they were free to do so—and God using their choices to accomplish His good intentions. We also see men and women believing in God through impossible circumstances and aligning themselves with God's intentions to redeem those who believe. Because of Jesus' resurrection, in the months and years that followed, many who formerly resisted God came to believe in Him. The event that looked like terrible failure and defeat became the cornerstone of faith and a glorious new victory.

Redeemed men and women can realign with the kingdom of God.

Although God's sovereign reign is not stymied by the power of human choice, this must not make us complacent about events or conditions in our fallen world. In other words, we must not sit back and say that God will make everything turn out all right in the end, so it doesn't matter what choices we make. We must never minimize the terribleness of sin or the power of righteousness. Rather, we must enter into God's loving and redemptive intentions. We are called (invited!) to line up heart and soul with the God who directs the universe toward His good purposes.

We live now in a tumultuous in-between. The power of Satan has been broken. The kingdom of Heaven is at hand. Jesus is the victor. God is about to break in and make all things new. Just as at the crucifixion, the darkness is thick and evil seems to be having its way—in economics, in politics, in international conflicts, in deception, in corruption, in exploitation, in hedonistic lifestyles. But God is on the move. He expects followers of His Son to live out—right now—His ways of righteousness for the new era.

So how do we live out the kingdom?

In recent years, this has become the focus of numerous books and seminars. I'm not going to try to evaluate what others are saying about the kingdom of God, but I'd like to throw out a caution. Through centuries of church history, this question has been asked and answered in a variety of ways, like waves coming and going, building up and finally breaking. In retrospect, we often have to hang our heads in embarrassment at misguided enthusiasm for "bringing it in." Think about the forced baptisms under Constantine and subsequent Roman rulers, the Crusades, wars during and after the Reformation, the Anabaptists at Münster, colonization efforts by numerous "Christian" nations, the witch trials in the New World, and postmillennial dreams in the nineteenth century. We haven't done so well at helping God bring in the kingdom, particularly when we resort to force, legislation, and other methods of this world.

I'd like to suggest two humble practices that Jesus and the apostles followed.

1. We need to pray forward God's intentions. Prayer is one of the mysteries of our interaction with the sovereign God. God is over everything and everyone all the time, but He invites us to ask Him to do things. He urges us not simply to wait on Him to do His great works, but to enter into the willing and working of restoring righteousness in our own lives and the lives of others.

As our hearts beat in rhythm with His great heart, we sorrow over sin and over the sinners. We allow our own hearts to be "touched with the feelings" of their sicknesses, failures, broken relationships, poverty, injustices, and weakness. This calls for engaging those around us, learning to know them, listening to their needs, and demonstrating the compassion of Jesus.

The brokenness and needs in our communities are bigger than we can manage. It is not difficult to get overwhelmed with human sorrow, to be very soon in over our heads. This calls us to prayer. We bring these needs to Jesus like the four men who carried the paralytic to Jesus. These guys weren't deterred by the crowds or the fact that Jesus was in the middle of a good sermon. They carried the man to the rooftop and opened up the roof to let him down in front of Jesus. Prayer is that kind of work. We are willing to "interrupt Heaven" with our requests. We do not quit until we have laid the need on holy ground at the throne of grace.

I do not mean that we can command God or that we can demand answers. Prayer is requesting—beseeching, asking, even begging. We never reverse roles with the One on the throne. There is but one sovereign. But we are assured that those who have given themselves to the mission of the King's business have been given direct audience with the King. He is the Sovereign, but we are His emissaries. We listen carefully to His instructions, memorize them, and make them our daily "to do" list. He listens to us—our reports, our sorrows and joys, our difficulties, our needs, and our concerns for others' needs. The jaw-dropping reality of prayer is that our requests move the heart and hand of the sovereign God.

2. We need to do good. The second way we live in the kingdom of God is to follow the example of Jesus and the apostles by serving people around us. When Peter spoke to a group of Gentiles at Cornelius's house, he summarized Jesus' life by saying He "went about doing good and healing all who were oppressed by the devil, for God was with Him" (Acts 10:38).

How did Jesus do this?

We find Jesus comforting those in sorrow, ministering to the sick, feeding the hungry, blessing the children, proclaiming the good news of His Father, teaching His followers how to live for the good of others, listening to people's woes, and offering hope. While Jesus proclaimed the Father's kingdom, amazingly He didn't initiate social or political programs. Most of his "doing good" was to individuals one-by-one, helping, healing, blessing, encouraging, forgiving, and comforting. When on occasion He fed the multitudes, those around Him saw the political and social potential and set out to make Him king by force. Jesus showed no interest.

We ought not to conclude that organizing ministry to groups of people is wrong. Soup kitchens, homeless shelters, rehab programs, counseling centers, pregnancy centers, kids clubs, and such ministries certainly line up with Jesus' ministry to relieve suffering and push against the tide of sin.

But two cautions: First, ministry is foremost about helping people, not running programs. Even a redeemed heart can easily be distracted from love for people and become focused on running a program. How easily followers of the humble Healer set out to build a ministry with their names and pictures splashed on the front pages of brochures. The prophet said this of Jesus:

> He will not cry out, nor raise His voice,
> Nor cause His voice to be heard in the street.
> A bruised reed He will not break,
> And smoking flax He will not quench.
> *Isaiah 42:2, 3; see also Matthew 12:19, 20*

Jesus Himself instructed us,

> Take heed that you do not do your charitable deeds before men, to be seen by them. Otherwise you have no reward from your Father in heaven. Therefore, when you do a charitable deed, do not sound a trumpet before you as the hypocrites do in the synagogues and in the streets, that they may have glory from men. Assuredly, I say to you, they have their reward. But when

> you do a charitable deed, do not let your left hand know what your right hand is doing, that your charitable deed may be in secret; and your Father who sees in secret will Himself reward you openly.
>
> *Matthew 6:1–4*

Doing good must not become a means of inflating our heads, building our kingdoms, or padding our nests. Rather, we are to do all to God's glory. Our goodness in daily interactions with people should point them to our Father, attracting them to His kindness and goodness. "Let your light so [in this manner] shine before men, that they may see your good works and glorify your Father in heaven" (Matthew 5:16).

The second caution about doing good to others is that the help we offer is not an end in itself. We are living out the righteousness of the new era as an announcement, as a proclamation of God's intention to make all things new. As we relieve the distressed, feed the poor, and give water to the thirsty, we both alleviate the miseries of this present system of sorrow and point people to the One who will bring in perfect righteousness. While we relieve the needs of the body, we invite people to quench the thirst of their souls, experience the forgiveness of their sins, and have their lives restored to wholeness in Jesus. On a small scale, we are participating in God's sovereign work to bring in the age of righteousness.

But we can't change the system. This present world is broken. We cannot bring in the new order through legislation, political power, or social systems. Even as we work for the good of those around us, we will not solve the core issues of this world system by improving the water, cleaning up the planet, wiping out diseases, redistributing wealth, or stopping the trafficking of children.

Christians who work to alleviate human distress may at times give more credence and attach more hope to their programs than those programs can actually deliver. We must guard against the expectation that changing people's circumstances will change their hearts and that changing their circumstances is the primary work God has given us to do.

We point people to the One who can change their lives at the core. Our good works point them to the One who has the authority and the capability to close this era of sin and usher in the era of righteousness. The God who orders the ages by His sovereign power and choice will do it in His time. By our kindness to broken people around us, we proclaim Him and invite them to trust Him through the smoke and din of a fallen system. We thus participate in His sovereign design while we wait for Him to make all things new.

WALKING WITH GOD

1. Acquaintance with the sovereign God should have at least two major effects on our hearts. First, it should curb our hankering to go down the path of disobedience—any such path is pointless, useless, and at best the long way home through much trouble and sorrow. We can never do anything outside of His full awareness and absolute ability to manage according to His good purposes. It is utterly foolish to try to run counter to God's purposes. Second, acquaintance with God's sovereignty should comfort our hearts because God is good. We will never be in a place or go through a situation that is outside the full awareness and rule of this great and loving God. To open your heart to God's sovereignty, read Psalm 115 and list your observations about who He is and how He operates.

2. Consider these examples of people who tried to live contrary to God's purposes and notice how He used their choices to accomplish His purposes:

    a. Pharaoh (Exodus 5–14), an extended example. God used Pharaoh's hard-hearted choices to bring disaster on Egypt as a consequence for their exploitation of the Israelites, to fund the Israelites' journey to Canaan, and to show both nations His sovereign power.

    b. Haman (Esther 3–7). When Haman disdained Mordecai and plotted to destroy the Jews, God instead assigned Haman, through the command of the king, to honor Mordecai publicly. Then God turned the day intended for the Jews' destruction into a day of deliverance.

    c. Caiaphas (John 11:49–53). This man, even while plotting Jesus' death, spoke a life-giving prophecy of the effectiveness of Jesus' death. All the efforts of the Jewish leaders to stop God's saving work through Jesus only resulted in accomplishing God's glorious intentions.

3. The following examples show people who at one point opposed God, but repented, chose to cooperate with Him, and moved from bondage to freedom.

    a. Manasseh (2 Chronicles 33). As we noted earlier, Manasseh was the most wicked king of Judah, dragging God's people into horrible sin. When he was imprisoned by the Babylonians, however, he repented and sought God's favor. As a result, God brought him back to his kingdom, where he attempted to bring good reforms.

    b. Jonah (Jonah 1–4). Jonah's disobedience and remarkable fish ride brought about his repentance and obedience. As a result, a heathen king and nation turned to God, leaving Jonah hot and bothered and wishing to die. This story is full of ironies, but note these expressions of God's sovereignty: "The LORD sent out a great wind" (1:4). "The LORD had prepared a great fish" (1:17). "The LORD God prepared a gourd" (4:6, KJV). "God prepared a worm" (4:7). "God prepared a vehement east wind" (4:8).

    c. Nebuchadnezzar (Daniel 4). This chapter was penned by a proud heathen king recounting how God humbled him. In spite of being warned, he gloried in his kingdom until God struck him with boanthropy, a condition in which he lived like a cow. He was booted from his throne as well as from human interaction until he learned a simple but profound truth—God reigns. His heartfelt praise of the God of Heaven at the end of his experience is inspiring.

    d. Saul (Acts 8:1–3; 9:1–22). Saul was a card-carrying Pharisee, determined to bring Jews back to obeying the Torah so the Messiah could come. N.T. Wright, commenting on Paul's references to being "zealous for God," writes: "We use the word 'zeal' to indicate warmth of heart and spirit, eagerness for a cause. That is a not inaccurate summary of one part of its first-century meaning, too. But whereas for the modern Christian 'zeal' is something you do on your knees, or in evangelism, or in works of charity, for the first-century Jew 'zeal' was something you did with a knife."[3] Saul terrorized the Christian community until he met Jesus on the road to Damascus. Not all the Greek manuscripts record the following words of Jesus. But He said something like, "Saul, it is not only hard on your toes but dangerous to your life to keep kicking like this against me—you are like an animal that keeps kicking against iron goads" (see Acts 9:5). The Amplified Bible translates it this way: "It is dangerous and it will turn out badly for you to keep kicking against the goad [to offer vain and perilous resistance]." Good, good advice!

4. God's sovereignty arches across the whole record of human history. The following are only samples for you to explore (and you may add your own examples). In your own words, tell how God's sovereignty was demonstrated in the following situations:

   a. When Adam and Eve sinned (Genesis 3)

   b. In Noah's time (Genesis 6–9)

   c. When the post-Flood people decided to build a tower (Genesis 11)

   d. In Jacob's life (Genesis 25, *ff.*)

   e. In the Exodus (Exodus 1–14)

   f. In Esther's life (Esther)

   g. In Daniel's life (Daniel)

   h. In Jesus' birth (Matthew 1, 2; Luke 1, 2)

   i. In Jesus' ministry (the Gospels)

   j. In Jesus' death and resurrection (Matthew 26–28)

   k. In the inclusion of the Gentiles (Acts 10; Romans 9–11)

5. Attempting to comprehend God's ability to run the world is a bit like attempting to comprehend the vastness and complexity of the universe. We get lost. But there is a very practical, heart-formative dimension to knowing the sovereign God. He is fully capable and completely trustworthy. Take some time to think about how His sovereignty can bring rest to your soul. After meditating, try to write out your thoughts.

Notes

1. Norman Geisler, *Chosen But Free* (Minneapolis: Bethany House Publishers, 1999), 54.

2. Randy Alcorn, "Do Human Beings Really Have Free Will?" *Eternal Perspectives* (Fall 2007): 1.

3. N. T. Wright, *What Saint Paul Really Said* (Grand Rapids: William B. Eerdmans Publishing Company, 1997), 27.

10

GOD IS RELATIONAL

Let Us make man in Our image,
according to Our likeness.

GENESIS 1:26

I and My Father are one.

JOHN 10:30

I do not pray for these alone,
but also for those who will believe in Me
through their word;
that they all may be one,
as You, Father, are in Me, and I in You;
that they also may be one in Us,
that the world may believe
that You sent Me.

JOHN 17:20, 21

The Trinity . . . the mystery thickens the further we go. In the beginning, God said, "Let Us make man in Our image." He didn't say, "I will;" He said, "Let us." But as He revealed Himself to His people, God insisted over and over He is one God, not many. "Hear, O Israel: The LORD our God, the LORD is one!" (Deuteronomy 6:4).

This declaration became the cornerstone of the Jewish faith. It was the first Scripture parents taught their children. They referred to it as the *shema*, meaning "hear," taken from the first word of the Hebrew text. "Hear! Pay careful attention to the truth of our God!" And what were they to hear? "The LORD, the LORD Jahweh, is our God. The Jahweh is one!"

In His oneness, Jehovah arrested His people again and again when they strayed into polytheism like the nations around them. Listen to His voice through Isaiah:

Thus says the LORD, the King of Israel,
And his Redeemer, the LORD of hosts:
"I am the First and I am the Last;
Besides Me there is no God."
Isaiah 44:6

"I am the LORD, and there is no other;
There is no God besides Me.
I will gird you, though you have not known Me,
That they may know from the rising of the sun to its setting
That there is none besides Me.
I am the LORD, and there is no other."
Isaiah 45:5, 6

For thus says the LORD,
Who created the heavens,
Who is God,
Who formed the earth and made it,
Who has established it,
Who did not create it in vain,
Who formed it to be inhabited:

"I am the Lord, and there is no other."
Isaiah 45:18

After centuries of hearing God's "oneness" and "no other" through the prophets, the Jews of Jesus' day understandably struggled when they heard Jesus say, "I and My Father are one" (John 10:30). There is one God. Even though Jesus' words affirmed that oneness, His hearers couldn't wrap their minds around two personalities in the one God.

Much less three! God the Father, God the Son, and God the Holy Spirit—the threesome in personality is not a departure from God's oneness, but neither does it seem rational. If someone were to tell us one plus one plus one equals one, we would assume he either hasn't made it through first grade or he has been reading so much Einstein he is relatively unhinged. And if we change the mathematical equation to one times one times one equals one, it only feels like we are playing games with terms.

It seems more honest to say we don't know how to explain it. Not that theologians haven't tried. The Athanasian Creed says:

> We worship one God in Trinity, and Trinity in Unity; neither confounding the persons, nor dividing the substance. For there is one Person of the Father, another of the Son, and another of the Holy Spirit. But the Godhead of the Father, of the Son, and of the Holy Spirit is all one, the glory equal, the majesty co-eternal. Such as the Father is, such is the Son, and such is the Holy Spirit. The Father uncreated, the Son uncreated, and the Holy Spirit uncreated; the Father incomprehensible, the Son incomprehensible, and the Holy Spirit incomprehensible; the Father eternal, the Son eternal, and the Holy Spirit eternal; and yet they are not three eternals, but one eternal. As also there are not three uncreated nor three incomprehensible, but one uncreated and one incomprehensible. So likewise the Father is almighty, the Son almighty, and the Holy Spirit almighty; and yet they are not three almighties,

> but one almighty. So the Father is God, the Son is God, and the Holy Spirit is God; and yet they are not three Gods, but one God. So likewise the Father is Lord, the Son Lord, and the Holy Spirit Lord; and yet they are not three Lords, but one Lord.

Analogies have been made to try to explain the three-in-one. Water, for example, appears in three forms—solid, liquid, and gas—but is still water in all three forms. An egg, for another example, is composed of an eggshell, an egg white, and an egg yolk, and all three make one egg. But these are only analogies, and like all analogies, they say only so much. If we put too much weight on them, like the eggs they make a mess that has to be cleaned up by more thoughtful theologians.

An early hymn dating back to the fourth century acknowledges the difficulty.

> Holy Father, Holy Son,
> Holy Spirit, three we name Thee;
> Though in essence only one,
> Undivided God we claim Thee,
> And adoring bend the knee,
> While we own the mystery!

God in triune oneness is beyond our understanding. We accept the oneness of God the Father, God the Son, and God the Holy Spirit by faith. God is above and beyond us in personality even as He is above and beyond us in everything else.

> You see, the doctrine of the Trinity, properly understood, is as much a way of saying 'we don't know' as of saying 'we do know'. To say that the true God is Three and One is to recognize that if there is a God then of course we shouldn't expect him to fit neatly into our little categories. If he did, he wouldn't be God at all, merely a god, a god we might perhaps have wanted. The Trinity is not something that the clever theologian

> comes up with as a result of hours spent in the theological laboratory, after which he or she can return to announce that they've got God worked out now, the analysis is complete, and here is God neatly laid out on a slab. The only time they laid God out on a slab he rose again three days afterwards. On the contrary: the doctrine of the Trinity is, if you like, a signpost pointing ahead into the dark, saying, 'Trust me; follow me; my love will keep you safe.' Or perhaps better, the doctrine of the Trinity is a signpost pointing into a light which gets brighter and brighter until we are dazzled and blinded, but which says: 'Come, and I will make you children of light.' The doctrine of the Trinity affirms the rightness, the propriety, of speaking intelligently about the true God, while at the same time affirming intelligently that the true God must always transcend our grasp of him, even our most intelligent grasp of him. As St. Paul says, what matters isn't so much our knowledge of God as God's knowledge of us; not, as it were, the god we want but the God who wants us. God help us, we don't understand ourselves; how can we expect to understand that Self which stands beside our selves like Niagara beside a trickling tap?[1]

Yes!

The members of the Trinity have distinct but interactive roles. We believe the Father and the Son and the Holy Spirit have unique roles, but that they are not separated in carrying them out. They live and work in such oneness it is easy to substitute one designation for the other, and yet the language of Scripture consistently assigns them distinctive roles. So the Father sent the Son into the world of material flesh, but Jesus in a human body was not separated from God the Father and God the Holy Spirit—the Father and His Spirit lived in Jesus in the world. In this way, we can say that the triune God came into humanity in the form of Jesus. Likewise, the Holy Spirit proceeds from the Father and the Son and was poured out on the believers in Jerusalem, but He was not and is not separated from the Father and the Son in that infusion of the church. So we believe the Father is among us and the Son is among us and in us when we are filled with the Holy Spirit.

The Father

Jesus the Son showed us the Father. God, as Father, is head of the family, begetting us and giving us grace to believe. In the order of God's workings, He sends the Son, and the Son assents to His will and accomplishes all that the Father sent Him to do. Likewise, the Father pours out His Spirit on believers, and we are filled with the Holy Spirit.

We note that Jesus instructs us to pray to the Father, to make our needs and requests known to Him, and to do so "in His name." He assures us the Holy Spirit will assist us in our praying. But the requests are addressed to the Father, not to the Son or to the Holy Spirit (although surely it is not inappropriate to speak to the Son or to the Holy Spirit as God, offering our praise, our worship, our deference, or even our desires). Thus we see the Father in an initiating, overseeing role.

The Son

Jesus the Son is the doer of the Father's will, active in creation, in redemption, and in the wrapping up of all the Father's good intentions for the world. "By Him all things were created" (Colossians 1:16). By His death and resurrection all that was ruined and destroyed by sin will be made alive and restored.

> Then comes the end, when He delivers the kingdom to God the Father, when He puts an end to all rule and all authority and power. For He must reign till He has put all enemies under His feet. The last enemy that will be destroyed is death. For 'He has put all things under His feet.' But when He says 'all things are put under Him,' it is evident that He who put all things under Him is excepted. Now when all things are made subject to Him,

> then the Son Himself will also be subject to Him who put all things under Him, that God may be all in all.
>
> *1 Corinthians 15:24–28*

Jesus came to earth to do the Father's will. He is at the center of the great work of redemption. He laid aside His glory to take on human form, and when His earthly ministry was done, He was received up again into glory. He sits at the Father's right hand and awaits the command to "come again," to complete the salvation of God's people, to usher in righteousness, and to "make all things new."

The Holy Spirit

God's Holy Spirit descends upon believers and brings into us the life and person of God. He makes us alive to God in the realm of the spirit, urging new life in our being—new thoughts, new feelings, new inclinations, new hopes, new perspectives, new orientation, new actions, new vocabulary (sometimes whole new languages), and new abilities. We do strange things when we come alive to God through the Spirit, and the more sinful our way of life was before faith, the more differently we behave. Filled with the Holy Spirit, we bless where we once cursed. We forgive heinous crimes and terrible people instead of hating and hurting in return. In Paul's words, in Christ we have become "a new creation" and "all things have become new" (2 Corinthians 5:17).

This is the Holy Spirit's work in us, but it is not separated from the Father and the Son. As Jesus said to His disciples in that last evening before His crucifixion, "I will pray the Father, and He will give you another Helper, that He may abide with you forever—the Spirit of truth." And shortly after, He added, "If anyone loves Me, he will keep My word; and My Father will love him, and We will come to him and make Our home with him" (John 14:16, 23).

The Spirit of God lives within us, showing us who Jesus is, teaching us that we are God's sons and daughters, encouraging us to call Him "Papa," speaking God's will to us, and then filling us with power to do more than we can do. It is sometimes almost more than a body can bear.

So God the Father is the one who initiates and sends. God the Son is the doer, the one who came among us to accomplish the Father's good pleasure. God the Holy Spirit is the infuser, coming into us, empowering us, and giving us the life and presence of the Father and the Son. But these three are one God, functioning in a oneness of being that defies full explanation.

It is tempting to try to imagine the divine interchange in the Trinity in an event such as the Creation. The Father wills to bring life in all its complexity out of nothing, and the Spirit is brooding over that expanse of nothingness, and the Son stands ready to bring materiality out of that nothingness. The Father gives the command, "Let there be light," and even as the command goes forth, the Son flings a gigantic mass of flaming light across the expanse, and the energizing Spirit shoots holy voltage into that light, and it explodes into galaxies by the billions! (No wonder it creates a run-on sentence!)

Suns and stars, giant reds, dwarf whites, black holes, gigantic comets, swirling masses, exploding and imploding clusters of energy, mass, and light! Big Bang, indeed! Was there a divine chuckle? A heavenly roar? Angels dancing nearby, whooping for joy? With that display of power (which with our telescopes we are only now appreciating), should it surprise us that the Holy Spirit falling upon a group of believers creates a little fireworks? More wonder that they weren't annihilated. (And no wonder at all that when the sons of Aaron tried to bring their own fire they did get annihilated.)

Well, that imaginative sketch of divine Trinity is shot through with a good deal of anthropomorphic fiction. We have only glimpses of what the members of the Trinity are really like and how they work in union. Their true working stretches beyond all human sight and knowing. But the astonishing reality is that this triune God lives within us, around us, above us, and beyond us, always working in perfect accord with Himself to bring about His good pleasure for the world.

The triune God lives and moves in perfect relationship.

God in three persons operates in continual, steadfast, and perfect love. God the Father, God the Son, and God the Holy Spirit plan in union, work in union, and love in union. They choose, fill, create, and complete in perfect union. There is communication within the Trinity, but no argument or contradiction. There is command—or declaration or willing—and there is response. Listen to the language Jesus used describing the relationship.

> "I can of Myself do nothing. As I hear, I judge; and My judgment is righteous, because I do not seek My own will but the will of the Father who sent Me."
>
> *John 5:30*

> "All that the Father gives Me will come to Me, and the one who comes to Me I will by no means cast out. For I have come down from heaven, not to do My own will, but the will of Him who sent Me."
>
> *John 6:37, 38*

> "If I do judge, My judgment is true; for I am not alone, but I am with the Father who sent Me."
>
> *John 8:16*

> "He who sent Me is with Me. The Father has not left Me alone, for I always do those things that please Him."
>
> *John 8:29*

> "If I do not do the works of My Father, do not believe Me; but if I do, though you do not believe Me, believe the works, that you may know and believe that the Father is in Me, and I in Him."
>
> *John 10:37, 38*

> "For I have not spoken on My own authority; but the Father who sent Me gave Me a command, what I should say and what I should speak. And I know that His command is everlasting life. Therefore, whatever I speak, just as the Father has told Me, so I speak."
>
> *John 12:49, 50*

Jesus reflects over and over the exchange between Himself and the Father—the Father speaking to Him, sending Him, commanding Him, and Jesus responding, doing the will of the Father continually.

God in the flesh certainly adds to the mystery. How could He who is Spirit become flesh and not become something other than Himself? How could the infinite take on finite form? How could omniscience and omnipresence shrink into the confines of time, space, and growth? Did Jesus have to learn like any other baby who grows into a child and adolescent? Did He develop the skills of carpentry through practice, through trial and error? Did He from childhood know the hearts of people, their thoughts, their desires, and their deepest motives? Or was that only as an adult, during His ministry?

Luke's Gospel records Jesus at the age of twelve already speaking of God the Father as His true Father and needing to be "about My Father's business" (Luke 2:49). In that same incident, we see the experts in the Law amazed at His answers. Later, we see the people "wondering" at His powerful teaching and even fearful of His might when He commanded demons and calmed the elements.

On the other hand, we find Jesus hungry, weary, and lonely. He was "in all points tempted as we are" (Hebrews 4:15). It is recorded that as an adolescent He "increased in wisdom" (Luke 2:52). Even as an adult He acknowledged limitations of His knowledge: "Of that day and hour no one knows, not even the angels in heaven, nor the Son, but only the Father" (Mark 13:32).

We don't have to figure it all out. On earth Jesus did the Father's will—living, moving, and working in perfect harmony with the Father's intentions by the power of the Holy Spirit.

The oneness of the Trinity informs the oneness of believers in Jesus. The night before Jesus was crucified, while He was still with His disciples, Jesus prayed for them. It is a profound prayer, showing us the heart of God the Son speaking to God the Father. As we overhear the interchange, the heart-stopping marvel is that we—yes, you and I, believers in the twenty-first century—are included in the prayer. Jesus talks to the Father about us!

> "I do not pray for these alone, but also for those who will believe in Me through their word; that they all may be one, as You, Father, are in Me, and I in You; that they also may be one in Us, that the world may believe that You sent Me. And the glory which You gave Me I have given them, that they may be one just as We are one: I in them, and You in Me; that they may be made perfect in one, and that the world may know that You have sent Me, and have loved them as You have loved Me."
>
> *John 17:20–23*

We are drawn into the oneness of the triune God! The unity of the Father, Son, and Spirit is to become the unity of us with them—and in them, us with one another. Coming into God's family through faith in His Son by the quickening Holy Spirit is bigger and better than we can imagine. We are coming into oneness with His plans, His decisions, His heart, His doings, and His living words. We come into His love, His holiness, His righteousness, His mercy, and His grace revealed in Jesus. He shares His life and nature with us—we have His DNA working steadily in us to produce His image in our speech, our actions and reactions, our bearing, the way we walk and respond, and the tone of our voice. In the words of Peter, we are "partakers of the divine nature" (2 Peter 1:5).

John explains it in even more detail:

> Little children, let no one deceive you. He who practices righteousness is righteous, just as He is righteous. He who sins is of the devil, for the devil has sinned from the beginning. For this purpose the Son of God was manifested, that He might destroy the works of the devil. Whoever has been born of God does not sin, for His seed remains in him; and he cannot sin, because he has been born of God.
>
> *1 John 3:7–9*

There you have it. The Father plants His seed (Greek, *sperma*—life seed, divine DNA, as it were) in His children, and His life works in us to produce right words and actions—a righteous walk. John is not teaching sinless perfection, but a changed way of life springing from the oneness we have with God. To be "born of God" is to begin living His way of life.

Being drawn into the life of God is to be drawn into divine fellowship. We talk and engage with the triune God in everyday living. We speak to Him about our work, our family relationships, our neighbors, our responsibilities, and our needs. It gets specific and down-to-earth—we talk about our baby's teething problems and fussy nights, about our neighbor's children who don't respect boundaries, about our parents' eccentricities as they get older, about the grumpy cashier we met, about family members and friends who are facing illness or distress, about the computer program that's giving us fits.

And we speak to God not only as individuals, but also in fellowship with other believers. When we get together, we talk to each other and pray about our personal ups and downs and the ways God met our needs, gave us encouraging verses, or brought us into conversation with a stranger struggling with cancer or divorce or loss of a job.

We live our lives together in fellowship with God. We see things the world does not see. We hear things. We know things. Together we share the joys and sorrows of living God's life in a broken world. John explains our interactions:

> That which was from the beginning, which we have heard, which we have seen with our eyes, which we have looked upon, and our hands have handled, concerning the Word of life—the life was manifested, and we have seen, and bear witness, and declare to you that eternal life which was with the Father and was manifested to us—that which we have seen and heard we declare to you, that you also may have fellowship with us; and truly our fellowship is with the Father and with His Son Jesus Christ.
>
> *1 John 1:1–3*

Our fellowship with God opens whole new dimensions to the way we see the world. We love it even as God "so loved the world," yearning to see people redeemed and rescued from sin and destruction, and like Him, willing to sacrifice toward that redemption. We "care for" the things of the world—our money, houses, work, possessions—in the context of carrying out God's intentions. We are not consumed with accumulating and protecting our stuff, anxious about the "cares of life." Rather we concern ourselves with using God's gifts in good ways, giving to those in need, relieving suffering, supporting God's servants, and partnering with fellow believers locally and around the world in missions, in ministries, in prison, and in persecution.

Our fellowship with God changes the way we see people. Paul says, "We regard no one according to the flesh" (2 Corinthians 5:16). With those who are "in the family" we share a special bond—brothers and sisters in Jesus. We don't have to try to create this bond. It's there, inherent in the holy conception. In the words of Paul again, we work to "keep the unity of the Spirit" (Ephesians 4:3). The key word is "keep." We work at preserving the oneness that is already given to us by the triune unity. From the beginning of the church, what we were before we believed is no determining factor to our coming in—fisherman, statesman, prostitute, tax collector, crook, priest, housewife, merchant, magician, single, married, Jew, Hispanic—all share in the oneness in Jesus. What we were "in the flesh" is superseded by who we become in Jesus. We are new creations in a new family.

In the new family, we are members joined in oneness to Him as well as "members one of another" (Ephesians 4:25, KJV). We not only receive this glorious new family identity of belonging to Him, but each one of us takes on new personal identity and function. One is a hand, one is an eye, one is the foot, and one is an internal organ whose work is unseen. But each member is divinely gifted to contribute to the others so that we "grow up" more and more "till we all come to the unity of the faith and of the knowledge of the Son of God, to a perfect man, to the measure of the stature of the fullness of Christ" (Ephesians 4:13).

Our union in Jesus works in us a union with each other, growing us up as individuals, but even more, making us as a people more like Him. "From [Him] the whole body, joined and knit together by what every joint supplies, according to the effective working by which every part does its share, causes growth of the body for the edifying of itself in love" (Ephesians 4:16).

This interaction and growth is sometimes overwhelmingly good, making us weep for joy and cry out in wonder. The worship, testimonies of God's goodness, confessions of failure and need, compassionate encouragement, praying together, passionate preaching, and close, small-group Bible studies fill our hearts to bursting with gratitude and love.

On the other hand, sometimes our interaction is downright messy. We have family fights and pouts and arguments and posturing that later make us ashamed at how cheerfully we have hurt one another. (We can especially see our folly and immaturity when removed by at least one generation from the spat—flabbergasted at how immature our fathers were.) Self-righteousness in the body of Jesus is a terrible cancer, looking and acting like healthy cell growth at first, but sucking life from the body all the while.

The Trinity has shared the divine life with us and pulled us together into oneness of heart and mind. Experiences of that unity through God's Spirit, like all the other experiences coming from His powerful anointing, shake us, thrill us, and deepen our longing for Him. But they are only foretastes. What we have now is a down payment, a guarantee. We are not yet living in the full reality of our redemption. Different New Testament writers say it in different ways. Paul describes our gathering into the oneness of Jesus and affirms that the Holy Spirit's presence among us is the "seal" of the Father's intentions to bring it all to perfection in the end.

> [God has] made known to us the mystery of His will, according to His good pleasure which He purposed in Himself, that in the dispensation of the fullness of the times He might gather together in one all things in Christ, both which are in heaven and which are on earth—in Him. . . . In Him you also trusted, after you

> heard the word of truth, the gospel of your salvation; in whom also, having believed, you were sealed with the Holy Spirit of promise, who is the guarantee of our inheritance until the redemption of the purchased possession, to the praise of His glory.
>
> *Ephesians 1:9, 10, 13, 14*

And John declares what we are now in Jesus is only a glimpse of what we will be.

> Behold what manner of love the Father has bestowed on us, that we should be called children of God! Therefore the world does not know us, because it did not know Him. Beloved, now we are children of God; and it has not yet been revealed what we shall be, but we know that when He is revealed, we shall be like Him, for we shall see Him as He is. And everyone who has this hope in Him purifies himself, just as He is pure.
>
> *1 John 3:1–3*

We don't always look like or feel like what we will be. Not by a Texas mile! But what the Father has begun is only the start of what He intends to do in us for His glory. We do well to focus more on our worship of this triune God and His amazing grace and on the call to "keep the unity" we receive in Him than on too eagerly pointing out to one another how we are not yet perfected.

WALKING WITH GOD

1. Even as God's sovereignty stretches beyond our understanding, so it is with the Trinity. From the earliest Biblical writers, we heard the strong (and uncommon for the time) declaration that God is one, and there is no other. In Jesus, we learned that the oneness in essence exists as a plurality in persons. ("I and My Father are one," John 10:30.) In the centuries since, we have tried in a variety of ways to understand and explain this divine reality. The explanations, like the understanding,

however satisfactory for the occasion, always fall short. Some explanations stray far enough wide of the mark that they have called for special councils and rigorous debates, resulting in finely-crafted statements. We may have different opinions about the accuracy or even the importance of these statements, but besides suggesting they always fall short, I'd like to point to one observation. Our best and clearest understandings of God as a plural oneness have come in community. I think that should give us both pause and humility—pause, lest we think too much of our personal explanations; humility, as we realize how much we need our friends in Christ in order to know Him. Simply stated, we understand God best when we experience Him together. This is why we must pay close attention to the "sharing time" or "testimony time" in any Christian community, whether it happens informally one-on-one or in the formal assembly. And to continue in real acquaintance with God, we must continually ask one another in some way, "How have you been experiencing God?" To carry this forward, you might try the following activities:

a. Think of your best friends one by one as you ask yourself the following questions: How have I experienced Jesus through Sandy? What have I learned about God through George? Try to write out specific responses to your questions.

b. Over the next days or weeks, ask your friends questions that enable them to talk about how they have experienced God. *What has God been saying to you recently? When you think of God the Father and Jesus, do you think differently of them? How do you think about Jesus and the Holy Spirit? What name of God has been the most meaningful to you, and why?* Be sure to let the conversations be honest, including their questions and struggles with God as well as their profound experiences.

2. Many of the classic hymns address the Trinity, some devoting one stanza each to the Father, Son, and Holy Spirit, sometimes followed by a fourth stanza addressing the Trinity. You are welcome to use one of the following older hymns or your own favorites, but read the text or sing the songs meditatively and worshipfully and let your heart experience fellowship. You might try singing these songs alone as well as with other believers. Record what you experience.

a. Come, Thou Almighty King,
Help us Thy name to sing,
Help us to praise:

Father, all-glorious,
O'er all victorious,
Come, and reign over us,
Ancient of Days.

Come, Thou Incarnate Word,
Gird on Thy mighty sword,
Our prayer attend:
Come, and Thy people bless,
And give Thy Word success;
Spirit of holiness
On us descend.

Come, Holy Comforter,
Thy sacred witness bear
In this glad hour:
Thou who almighty art,
Now rule in every heart,
And ne'er from us depart,
Spirit of power.

To the great One in Three
Eternal praises be
Hence evermore.
His sovereign majesty
May we in glory see,
And to eternity
Love and adore.

—Robert Robinson

b. Eternal Father, when to Thee,
Beyond all worlds, by faith I soar,
Before Thy boundless majesty
I stand in silence, and adore.

But, Savior, Thou art by my side;
Thy voice I hear, Thy face I see:
Thou art my Friend, my daily Guide;
God over all, yet God with me.

And Thou, great Spirit, in my heart
Dost make Thy temple day by day;

The Holy Ghost of God Thou art,
Yet dwellest in this house of clay.

Blest Trinity, in whom alone
All things created move or rest,
High in the heav'ns Thou hast Thy throne;
Thou hast Thy throne within my breast.

—Hervey Ganse

c. Holy, holy, holy! Lord God Almighty!
Early in the morning our song shall rise to Thee;
Holy, holy, holy! Merciful and mighty!
God in three persons, blessed Trinity!

Holy, holy, holy! All the saints adore Thee,
Casting down their golden crowns around the glassy sea;
Cherubim and seraphim falling down before Thee,
Which wert, and art, and evermore shalt be.

Holy, holy, holy! Though the darkness hide Thee,
Though the eye of sinful man Thy glory may not see;
Only Thou art holy; there is none beside Thee
Perfect in power, in love, and purity.

Holy, holy, holy! Lord God Almighty!
All Thy works shall praise Thy name, in earth, and sky, and sea;
Holy, holy, holy! Merciful and mighty,
God in three persons, blessed Trinity!

—Reginald Heber

d. Holy God, we praise Thy Name;
Lord of all, we bow before Thee;
All on earth Thy scepter claim,
All in heav'n above adore Thee.
Infinite Thy vast domain,
Everlasting is Thy reign.

Hark, the loud celestial hymn,
Angel choirs above are raising;
Cherubim and seraphim,
In unceasing chorus praising,

Fill the heav'ns with sweet accord:
Holy, holy, holy Lord.

Lo! the apostolic train
Join Thy sacred name to hallow;
Prophets swell the glad refrain,
And the white-robed martyrs follow;
And, from morn to set of sun,
Through the church the song goes on.

Holy Father, Holy Son,
Holy Spirit, three we name Thee;
Though in essence only one,
Undivided God we claim Thee,
And adoring bend the knee,
While we own the mystery.

—The words of this hymn come from the late fourth century.

3. Following are a variety of biblical texts to explore. In a variety of ways, they indicate the love and oneness in the three persons of the Trinity.

   a. "Let Us make man in Our image, according to Our likeness. . . . So God created man in His own image; in the image of God He created him; male and female He created them" (Genesis 1:26, 27).

   b. "Go therefore and make disciples of all the nations, baptizing them in the name of the Father and of the Son and of the Holy Spirit" (Matthew 28:19).

   c. "If you had known Me, you would have known My Father also. . . . You are from beneath; I am from above. You are of this world; I am not of this world. . . . When you lift up the Son of Man, then you will know that I am He, and that I do nothing of Myself; but as My Father taught Me, I speak these things. And He who sent Me is with Me. The Father has not left Me alone, for I always do those things that please Him" (John 8:19, 23, 28, 29).

   d. "I and My Father are one" (John 10:30).

   e. "If you had known Me, you would have known My Father also; and from now on you know Him and have seen Him. . . . He who has seen Me has seen the Father" (John 14:7, 9).

f. "And I will pray the Father, and He will give you another Helper, that He may abide with you forever—the Spirit of truth, whom the world cannot receive, because it neither sees Him nor knows Him; but you know Him, for He dwells with you and will be in you. . . . But the Helper, the Holy Spirit, whom the Father will send in My name, He will teach you all things, and bring to your remembrance all things that I said to you" (John 14:16, 17, 26).

g. "But when the Helper comes, whom I shall send to you from the Father, the Spirit of truth who proceeds from the Father, He will testify of Me" (John 15:26).

h. "The grace of the Lord Jesus Christ, and the love of God, and the communion of the Holy Spirit be with you all" (2 Corinthians 13:14).

4. Acquaintance with the Father, Son, and Holy Spirit is an experience in fellowship. As John describes it: "The life was manifested, and we have seen, and bear witness, and declare to you that eternal life which was with the Father and was manifested to us—that which we have seen and heard we declare to you, that you also may have fellowship with us; and truly our fellowship is with the Father and with His Son Jesus Christ" (1 John 1:2, 3). Compare this description with the records of Christian fellowship in the early chapters of Acts.

Notes

1. N. T. Wright, *For All God's Worth* (Grand Rapids: William B. Eerdmans Publishing Company, 1997), 24-25.

GOD IS OMNIPOTENT

And the LORD said to Abraham,
"Why did Sarah laugh, saying,
'Shall I surely bear a child, since I am old?'
Is anything too hard for the LORD?"

GENESIS 18:13, 14

Ah, LORD GOD!
Behold, You have made the heavens and the earth
by Your great power and outstretched arm.
There is nothing too hard for You.

JEREMIAH 32:17

With God nothing will be impossible.

LUKE 1:37

We've heard and read and sung the truth of God's omnipotence enough to know it forward and backward. But when it comes to our own experiences, we have a terrible time believing it. We read the stories in the Bible. As children, we loved them. As adults, we tell them, but sometimes without the open-eyed wonder we had when we were young.

But the gracious truth remains. God can do anything. Nothing is beyond His ability.

Let's get a couple of qualifiers aside immediately. God cannot sin. And as the song says, "God can do anything but fail." Furthermore, when we say God can do anything, we don't mean He does things logically inconsistent with reality. So the favorite question in this regard is the one adolescents love to ask: Can God make something so heavy He can't lift it? Okay. It's also pointless to ask if God can make a square circle. Or if He could make happiness purple. Or if He could tell a true lie. Such conundrums aside, let's explore omnipotence.

God can make the world out of nothing, just by saying it should appear. If He can do that, He can also part the sea, make walls fall down, multiply food, create new food, send a storm to a specific location on the spur of the moment (or calm it), make a day last forty-eight hours, heal the sick, and raise the dead. God can do whatever He wants.

This kind of power is terrifying from a human vantage point. As Lord Acton said centuries ago, "Power corrupts. Absolute power corrupts absolutely." In the hands of humans, power turns septic. We use it to put down opposition at whatever level, at whatever cost, by whatever method it takes to win. We use it to control, manipulate, and oppress, ostensibly, of course, to "keep order."

Our use of power, even when at first intended for good purposes, easily turns self-serving. We can split the atom to produce electricity, and we can split it to liquidate cities, incinerate its citizens, and blind and maim its survivors. We can program our computers to calculate and sort and transmit zillions of communications every second, and we can program them to navigate drones that blast and kill halfway around the world from the controller in his air-conditioned office. We can use our gases and chemicals to exterminate pests and weeds, we can package our concoctions as medicines to fight disease, and we can use these same chemicals to exterminate unwanted people groups in gas chambers. In the hands of humans, power looks so attractive, but it seems inevitably to bend toward horrifying uses.

With God, absolute power is joined to His absolute goodness, to His perfect righteousness, to His pure holiness, to His committed love—to all that is God. He exercises His power to bring about redemption and righteousness and to purge the world of evil. Doing this good work in a wicked world is His glory, His signature expression of ability and goodness and power.

Ironically, here is where we often stumble. We judge God's use of power from the vantage point of local incidents, personal discomfort, or immediate situations. When we step on a nail and experience pain, when we have anything from a headache to a terminal illness, when we don't have the money to pay a bill, when a friend or spouse lets us down, when a member of our family is wounded or raped or killed . . . and when God doesn't prevent or solve these troubles for us, we judge Him as either impotent or uncaring. If God has all that power and He loves people, He ought to use His power to prevent evil and rescue good people. If galaxies appeared at His word and devils fled at His command, why can't He get us out of the scrapes and hassles of daily living?

God uses His power to accomplish His intentions.

I am not big enough or smart enough to explain God's choices in the use of His power, but I've concluded a couple of things. First, God does not intend to make His power available to accomplish all our local, personal, and parochial whims. Jesus' invitation to His disciples to "ask anything" in His name and the Father would do it needs context. Imagine the chaos if every person, even every Christian, had an automatic hook-up to omnipotence. One would call for rain because he just seeded his lawn, and his next-door neighbor might be calling for sunshine the same morning because he wants to eat sandwiches in the park. One church member would be praying for funds for a church expansion, and his brother (maybe even his fellow church trustee) might be praying that the church would abandon this silly project. We are a bit short-sighted and a tad too self-interested to be given the right to sling around omnipotence.

Second, God uses His power to carry forward His intentions. This use of His power has a number of strands we need to tease out. Right down the middle of God's omnipotence is His glory. God is the center of reality, the hub of all existence, beauty, and significance. Every molecule of the world quivered with His glory in Creation. But when we sinned, we fell short of the glory of God and fell into the darkness and destruction of our own ways. Our sin turned even the dance of the molecules into groaning.

God's glory is restored, then, in redemption. Currently this is at work in redeeming people who trust in Him. This is His intent. (Ultimately, that intention will purge the whole system of evil and restore perfect righteousness and joy, even in the molecules.) So the mega-story of God's doings in the world is filled with episodes of God bringing us back, and in those redemptive episodes His power does what only God can do. He calls, He rescues, He reveals Himself, He speaks, He heals, He restores, He corrects and punishes, and He forgives. He does all this with power and authority, but always with the goal of restoring us to Himself and redeeming a people "to the praise of His glory" (Ephesians 1:12, see also vv. 6 and 14).

When we come to God, repenting of our ways and coming back into His ways, we experience His power. The hand that grips us exudes omnipotence, and our stories of coming back always reflect this. That's why we love to hear them. The puzzled Ethiopian officer "happened" to be reading about Jesus in Isaiah when Philip met him . . . Paul got knocked off his donkey by a white laser beam before laser was discovered . . . A former KGB officer is converted and is now a preacher . . . A stripper miraculously gets saved and dedicates her life to reaching other strippers . . . Yes, that's a story I read just recently.

Anny Donewald was a stripper, and one day she heard this "voice" say to her: "Matthew four-sixteen." Anny was not a Bible reader. She asked her sister, "Who the [blank] is Matthew?" (We even pardon such language when omnipotence is on the move.) Her sister pointed her to the Bible, and Anny read, "The people dwelling in darkness have seen a great light, and for those dwelling in the region and shadow of death, on them a light has dawned" (ESV). Anny began weeping, was led to repentance, received Jesus, and today she reaches out to other strippers with her story of redemption.

There you have it—God's power working for His glory, accomplishing His redemptive purposes.

We must align our lives with God's purposes to experience His power.

Whenever and wherever we align ourselves with God's redemptive work, all along the cutting edge of that work we will experience God's power. God will take illiterate men and women and give them a voice that rattles the most educated. (K. P. Yohannan, for example, didn't wear shoes until he was seventeen, but he has become one of the most influential voices of faith to India as well as to many in the U.S.) God takes people from the ugliest sector of human experience—sex trade, crime, drug addiction—and transforms them and gives them a ministry. (Nicky Cruz was a street druggie and a gang leader before becoming an evangelist who has led thousands to Jesus.)

Even as God's power changes lives, it also works on behalf of His children who cry out to Him for help, healing, guidance, and the whole range of human need. Every child of God engaged in God's work has stories of divine intervention. God gives food and money—sometimes down to the exact dollar amount. God brings two people together from opposite corners of the world at the precise moment necessary to show His guidance. God uses a stranger (or even an unbeliever) to speak the exact words a believer needs to hear to be encouraged. These examples of power—God-moments, God-things, if you please—happen over and over. But I'm saying again, they happen especially along the cutting edge of the story going forward into new territory, bringing new believers into the family.

A. B. Simpson, a preacher from a century ago, tells the story of his miraculous healing. For more than twenty years he suffered from a weak heart, resulting in a variety of physical ailments and limiting his studies and activities. Even climbing a flight of stairs would leave him feeling suffocated and in pain. After delivering a sermon, it was common him to be so exhausted that he rested until the middle of the week when he needed to begin preparing the sermon for the next Sunday.

One summer when by a doctor's orders he was convalescing at a campground, he found himself discouraged and deeply distressed. In his depression he was wandering about the campground when he heard the sound of a group singing the simple words of a spiritual: "My Jesus is the Lord of lords: No man can work like Him."

Simpson recalls, "It seemed like a voice from heaven. It possessed my whole being." He became convinced that God wanted to heal him, so he went into a pine woods, raised his right hand to heaven, and pledged to trust Jesus alone for his healing and health from that day forward.

Simpson was completely healed and later wrote, "Thanks be to God, the first three years after I was healed I preached more than a thousand sermons, and held sometimes more than twenty meetings in one week, and do not remember once feeling exhausted." For thirty-five years after his healing, he continued to preach, during which time he founded Christian and Missionary Alliance, one of the largest mission organizations in the world.[1]

It is easy, then, when we experience these God-moments, to assume that this is what God's power is all about. Since God did a miracle to save us or to provide for us in a certain situation, we consider that to be the singular evidence of God or the primary purpose of His power. We have a knack for being short-sighted. We live today. Yesterday, when we last experienced that God-thing was a long time ago. Without realizing it, we let our faith shift from God to the signs. We come to rely on a tangible God-moment to verify that God is still around and breathing. So if we pray for a miracle and it doesn't happen, or if we learn we have a disease and He doesn't heal, or if we lose something valuable that He doesn't locate, we jump to some very unhealthy conclusions: God is absent rather than present. He isn't paying very good attention to our prayers. He doesn't care. He isn't as healthy and well as we thought He was.

Like children, we have assumed that the primary use of God's power and resources is to solve our problems. Without realizing it, we have been operating as though we, rather than He, stood at the center of the universe.

God's intentions, and thus His mighty works, often extend beyond our understanding.

We must tease out another strand in understanding omnipotence: Because God's omnipotent power flows through His intentions, His works are always beyond our full understanding.

> "For My thoughts are not your thoughts,
>   Nor are your ways My ways," says the LORD.
> "For as the heavens are higher than the earth,
>   So are My ways higher than your ways,
> And My thoughts than your thoughts."
>
> *Isaiah 55:8, 9*

God is God. When God's power is at work, it is pushing forward purposes we cannot fully comprehend. This does not mean they do not involve us or that we cannot see *anything* about His intentions. Often we clearly see good things God is doing. The eternal truth is that always in every situation He is working for the good of those who love Him. But the ways He goes about answering our prayers and exercising His incredible power and fulfilling those good intentions may look to us like an unanswered prayer exactly because He is doing something bigger than we asked for.

When the Israelites were suffering in Egypt, they cried out to God. At a time when Israelite babies were being fed to the crocodiles in the Nile, His answer was to give them a baby. Get this: The order to throw them into the river was from Pharaoh, and God arranged for the future leader of His people to be rescued and cared for by Pharaoh's daughter. (God's power is also linked to His sense of humor, by the way. See Psalm 2.) The point here is that when it seemed like God was doing nothing, as though the prayers for deliverance were going unanswered year after year, God was doing something bigger than what the Israelites were asking for.

Eighty years later (eighty years, mind you, when many of the first to pray for deliverance were dead and gone), Moses led the Israelites out of Egypt in terrifying demonstrations of divine power. These stupendous acts of God were intended to demonstrate before all people God's power and glory in deliverance as well as the stupidity of trying to work against omnipotence. Furthermore, God used the harshness of their living conditions in Egypt to forge them into a people of faith and prepare them to trust and follow Him as no nation ever had in human history.

The story of Israel's deliverance from Egypt has become the prototype of salvation stories. Ever since then (even with the change of covenants), God's people speak and sing of coming out of our own Egypt.

Examples of God's higher ways abound in Scripture. The story of why the Israelites were in Egypt began with Joseph. He was hated by his brothers and sold as a slave to an Egyptian officer. God's power sustained Joseph, not taking him out of trouble (even allowing it to get worse), but still working toward bigger purposes than Joseph could understand. At the right time, God brought Joseph out of prison and made him second-in-command over Egypt. God used Joseph to preserve his family—to do good to his brothers as a way of humbling their hearts. God was redeeming Joseph, although to Joseph it likely seemed to be taking a long time and his prayers seemed to be going unanswered, but God was also redeeming Joseph's brothers. On an even bigger scale, God was already setting the stage to redeem His people.

We should note that suffering is a common ingredient in God's work of redemption. When we call on God to use His power on our behalf, we are focused primarily on getting ourselves out of our scrap. That's what we think of as divine power—blinding or incapacitating those who intend to do evil, sending angels to clear the way, dropping the money we need right out of the stratosphere, and shooting a little heavenly chemo into our bodies to zap the sickness and confound the doctors.

I'm not saying God never does these things. He can do what He pleases. But redemption is more than getting us out of trouble. It often includes getting some deeply embedded trouble out of ourselves. And purifying is seldom easy or quick. In the Bible we see God regularly including personal suffering in the experiences of His favorite characters, even while He is doing astounding things through them. His intention is not to make them miserable, but to make them pure. Thus we are convinced Joseph was a better ruler as a result of his years of mistreatment, injustice, and imprisonment. David was a wiser and more merciful king exactly because he was chased around the country by his maniacal father-in-law. Ruth the Moabite became a woman of faith, virtue, and loyalty through the loss of her husband and her ensuing life of poverty and hardship. The writer to the Hebrews first quotes from the Psalms to make this point and then explains it in more detail:

> And you have forgotten the exhortation which speaks to you as to sons:
>
> > "My son, do not despise the chastening of the LORD,
> > Nor be discouraged when you are rebuked by Him;
> > For whom the LORD loves He chastens,
> > And scourges every son whom He receives."
>
> If you endure chastening, God deals with you as with sons; for what son is there whom a father does not chasten? But if you are without chastening, of which all have become partakers, then you are illegitimate and not sons. Furthermore, we have had human fathers who corrected us, and we paid them respect. Shall we not much more readily be in subjection to the Father of spirits and live? For they indeed for a few days chastened us as seemed best to them, but He for our profit, that we may be partakers of His holiness. Now no chastening seems to be joyful for the present, but painful; nevertheless, afterward it yields the peaceable fruit of righteousness to those who have been trained by it.
>
> *Hebrews 12:5–11*

To reiterate this particular line of thought: God's power is exercised in behalf of His people according to His wise and good (and gigantic!) intentions. We must not abandon our trust in His capability or His love when it seems to us He is not doing what we ask. We can assume something bigger and better is happening than what we asked for, or that He has purposes that we cannot presently understand.

God is able to turn the works of evil into the means of accomplishing His intentions.

This brings us to yet another strand in the incredible working of God's power. In exercising His power to deliver and redeem and purify His people, God turns evil on its head. He does this in a variety of ways. He uses what comes to us as evil to do good things. He uses weakness in us, for example, to make us strong. Or He uses tragedy to deepen our love and increase our joy. He turns loss into riches. Through pain and adversity, He teaches us and purifies us and makes us beautiful, loving, faithful, and wise.

Through God's mighty power, sickness, tragedy, loss, and even death itself are stripped of their power to harm us. Yes, we can give testimonies of God sparing us from these things. But if God's power always kept us from trouble, wouldn't many people come to God only for an easier life—no disease or pain, nobody hurt, everybody wealthy and smiling and trouble-free? This was not the experience of the early Christians, nor has it been the experience of the godly through the centuries. If anything, we seem to get more than our share of trouble. But through the working of God's power on our behalf, these earthly sorrows lose their strength to do us any lasting harm; instead they are the means by which we become strong and holy and rich in Him.

> Who shall separate us from the love of Christ? Shall tribulation, or distress, or persecution, or famine, or nakedness, or peril, or sword? As it is written:
>
> "For Your sake we are killed all day long;
> We are accounted as sheep for the slaughter."
>
> Yet in all these things we are more than conquerors through Him who loved us. For I am persuaded that neither death nor life, nor angels nor principalities nor powers, nor things present nor things to come, nor height nor depth, nor any other created thing, shall be able to separate us from the love of God which is in Christ Jesus our Lord.
>
> *Romans 8:35–39*

The greatest demonstration of God's power in this regard was when they crucified Jesus. Notice that even Jesus prayed for deliverance—prayed in such agony of spirit that He sweated blood. "Let this cup pass from me!" So it's not wrong to pray that God would use His power to spare us from suffering and get us out of trouble. But Jesus couched His prayer in submission to the Father, and the Father's will was for His Son to drink the cup of suffering and death.

Was Jesus' prayer answered? The writer to the Hebrews says, "In the days of His flesh, when He had offered up prayers and supplications, with vehement cries and tears to Him who was able to save Him from death, [He] was heard because of His godly fear" (5:7). His prayer was heard!

The Father was able to save His Son from death (literally, "out from within"), and that's exactly what He did. He let the soldiers beat and whip and crucify His Son. He let His Son die. And when Jesus was "down in death," the Father resurrected Him, ripping to shreds the bonds of death and evil. The blow that fell on Jesus' back broke the powers of evil. By going down into death in weakness, He was enabled to rise up from death in power, thereby sealing the doom of Satan and all his hosts. "Inasmuch then as the children have partaken of flesh and blood, He Himself likewise shared in the same, that through death He might destroy him who had the power of death, that is, the devil, and release those who through fear of death were all their lifetime subject to bondage" (Hebrews 2:14, 15).

Writing to the Colossians, Paul said it this way: "Having disarmed principalities and powers, He made a public spectacle of them, triumphing over them in it" (2:15). God uses His power again and again to turn evil on its head.

We see this power of God at work when we trust Him. God used Stephen's death to help bring about the conversion of early Christianity's most notorious persecutor. God used the scattering of the church (by Saul's diabolical hatred) to spread the news of Jesus far and wide. God used the sufferings of Peter and Paul and the other apostles to strengthen the message of the Gospel, to encourage believers that it is an honor to share in the suffering of Jesus, and to turn their sorrow into joy. God used the jailing of Paul and Silas to bring about the jailer's conversion and strengthen the church at

Philippi. He used Paul's later imprisonment to produce letters that would be preserved to help guide the church through the centuries. God used John's exile to give us the Revelation. (By the way, God has brought marvelous writings to His people over and over from the pens of saints either while they were in prison or after they came out. John Bunyan gave us *The Pilgrim's Progress*, Alexander Solzhenitsyn wrote the *Gulag Archipelago,* Dietrich Bonhoeffer penned *Community,* Richard Wurmbrand wrote *Tortured for Christ,* and Corrie ten Boom gave us *The Hiding Place*.) Whenever the forces of evil make advances, we are called to place our faith in God's mighty power, and God uses their very advances to defeat them. He turns evil on its head.

God's people present this enigma to the watching world. We are weak. We are often defenseless. We are mostly nobodies. But we are following One who is all-powerful. By Him we are led and protected. By Him our needs are met. And against all odds, we go forward exactly in the places where we seem to be defeated, overthrown, and cast down.

To God's enemies, this has proved to be maddening. To those whose eyes are trained on Heaven, the working of His power is cause for continual eruptions of praise.

In the fog of this world, when we are abandoned and hurting, when nothing powerful seems to be happening, it is easy to lose sight of the omnipotence that surrounds us and is working on our behalf. We need to pray for each other and offer encouragement to those who are in the throes of trial, as Paul prayed for the Ephesian Christians:

> I . . . do not cease to give thanks for you, making mention of you in my prayers: that the God of our Lord Jesus Christ, the Father of glory, may give to you the spirit of wisdom and revelation in the knowledge of Him, the eyes of your understanding being enlightened; that you may know what is the hope of His calling, what are the riches of the glory of His inheritance in the saints, and what is the exceeding greatness of His power toward us who believe, according to

the working of His mighty power which He worked in Christ when He raised Him from the dead and seated Him at His right hand in the heavenly places, far above all principality and power and might and dominion, and every name that is named, not only in this age but also in that which is to come.

Ephesians 1:15–21

WALKING WITH GOD

1. Consider the following examples of people in the Bible encountering God's power. How do these stories deepen your love for God? How do they strengthen your faith?
   a. God told Gideon his army was too large, stripping it from 32,000 (against a Midianite army too numerous to count) down to a measly 300 men (Judges 7).
   b. God sent fire from Heaven to burn a drenched sacrifice, lick up the water, and consume the stones of the altar (1 Kings 18).
   c. God completely diffused the power of an incredibly hot fire for three young men who dared to honor Him in the face of a raging heathen king (Daniel 3).
   d. Jesus cured a leper, healed a paralyzed man from a distance, healed Peter's mother-in-law, commanded a storm to stop, and drove demons out of a man, permitting them to enter a herd of pigs (Matthew 8).
2. What are your favorite Bible stories of God's power? List a few and for each one try to put into words what the story reveals about God's power.
3. Why do you think it is difficult for people today to believe in God's omnipotence?
4. In your observation, how do people attempt to use the power of God for their own ends?

5. Read Psalm 111 and write down everything the psalmist says about God's "works." What have been your own encounters with the Almighty? Write out the details of one or two encounters as clearly as you can remember them. Arrange to tell your story to someone, either one-on-one or to a group (such as during a family worship time or church testimony time).
6. What songs about God's power are especially meaningful to you? Write the lyrics and tell why they mean so much to you.

Notes

1. A. B. Simpson, *The Gospel of Healing*, rev. ed. (1915; repr., Harrisburg, PA: Christian Publications, Inc., n.d.), 154.

GOD IS OMNISCIENT

O Lord, You have searched me and known me.
You know my sitting down and my rising up;
You understand my thought afar off.
You comprehend my path and my lying down,
And are acquainted with all my ways.
For there is not a word on my tongue,
But behold, O Lord, You know it altogether.
You have hedged me behind and before,
And laid Your hand upon me.
Such knowledge is too wonderful for me;
It is high, I cannot attain it.

PSALM 139:1–6

I have a distinct boyhood memory of my cousins telling about coming home to a disturbing scene. As they stepped through the door, they saw the contents of their house scattered everywhere. Drawers had been emptied, doors left open, contents of cupboards and closets and dressers strewn around in jumbled wreckage. The realization shot through their racing minds: "We've been robbed!"

As I recall, the actual loss was not that significant—a small amount of cash and a few guns. But what haunted their minds for months and raced at odd moments down pathways of raw nerves was the sense of invasion. Someone had intruded into their private lives—had walked into their personal space, looked at and fingered and then trashed very personal possessions. The lingering unease was not only that someone had seen them and now knew things about them at a very personal and private level, but also that their experience of being ravaged had taken place at the hands of others altogether. My cousins lived with the grim and terrifying awareness that they had no consent and little control over whether or when it could happen again.

God knows everything about us.

Meditating on God's greatness, King David became aware that God knew him, not from the outside as someone observing and interacting with him, but inside out. We are not told what led to this realization. Had David done something shameful or sinful? Was he contemplating something he didn't want anyone to know about? Had he gone somewhere? Met someone? Gotten into trouble?

For some reason, the realization of God's omniscience hit him hard. Gasp! *He knows what I'm thinking! He sees everything I do! He knows my habits—the ones people see and the ones I keep hidden! He listens to my private mutterings. He is fully aware of everything in my heart, down to the most secret motivations. He knows not only what I do and say but what I'd like to do and say, what I dream about, what I want people to see and what I don't want them to see. And I can't get away from Him. There's nowhere to go where He is not already there ahead of me. There's no time of the day or night when I can be by myself. Every detail of my life is strewn out in plain sight before Him. I have no privacy!*

"Lord, You have searched me and known me." The Hebrew word translated *searched* is stronger than most English translations. "You have ransacked me," would be closer. Searched thoroughly! Investigated! Sorted through! The complete searching informs the complete knowing. The Hebrew word *yada*, translated *know*, is a broad term, but is usually associated with intimate knowing, acquaintance at a deep level.

Such knowledge does not always comfort us. It can make us squirm uncomfortably. Our instinctive reaction may be to bolt. But that does us no good before the All-Knowing.

If I ascend into heaven, You are there;
  If I make my bed in hell, behold, You are there.
If I take the wings of the morning,
  And dwell in the uttermost parts of the sea,
Even there Your hand shall lead me,
  And Your right hand shall hold me.
If I say, "Surely the darkness shall fall on me,"
  Even the night shall be light about me;
Indeed, the darkness shall not hide from You,
  But the night shines as the day;
  The darkness and the light are both alike to You.
    Psalm 139:8–12

Omniscience requires omnipresence. If God knows everything, then God is present with us everywhere in all events at all times. He is thoroughly acquainted with our history as well as everything going on right now around us and within us down to the most hidden intent of our hearts. The really unnerving part about God knowing everything about us is that He is more accurate in His understanding of us than we are ourselves. When we think we are strong and capable, He knows the exact place and time and circumstances where we will falter.

After Peter's denial, when Jesus asked him the third time, "Do you love me?" the realization of being known deep down to the core cut to the quick. The Gospel writer records, "Peter was hurt because Jesus asked him the third time, 'Do you love me?' He said, 'Lord, you know all things; you know that I love you'" (John 21:17, NIV). Ouch. "You know the weakness of my heart. You know the imperfections of my love, the shortness of my devotion, the shame of my denial. But such as it is, I do love you."

To be searched out and found out, having not a shred of cover, can be excruciating. For Peter, it stabbed deeply. For David, it was overwhelming: "Such knowledge is too wonderful for me!"

God's knowing is joined to His infinite love.

David doesn't stop there. "For you formed my inward parts," he says. "You knitted me together in my mother's womb" (v. 13, ESV). This

God not only knew him thoroughly, but also had designed him and had put him together. "You fashioned me, constructed my bones and muscles and tendons and tissue. You threaded the strands of my DNA, wove them together to make me who I am. You are my Maker, my personal designer."

This realization of God's "ransacking" departs widely from the terror of being ransacked by robbers. Robbers invade what does not belong to them; God knows us intimately because we are His. The robbers' intent is to plunder and steal; God's intent is to purify and redeem. The robbers' invasion violates and devalues who we are; God searches us out because He loves us, and His love validates who we are.

In human relationships our loving is limited to our knowing. Sanctified as it may sound to say we love everyone in the world, we can't really love people halfway around the world without any acquaintance with them. If we read about a hidden tribe in a remote area of the world, that very minimal understanding may move our hearts to have compassion, perhaps to give money for their needs, maybe even to raise funds, or ultimately to go to them in person. But the depth of our love will depend upon the extent of the acquaintance. Understanding *about* someone is not equal to acquaintance *with* someone. As we sit with, talk with, listen to, care for, sacrifice for, and feel with people, our acquaintance with them gives us the raw material needed to build a relationship. Reading fliers or news snippets won't give us the level of love for a people group that we would possess after living five years among them. Or to change the scene, we certainly can have love—blissful love—at the wedding altar, but we cannot at that moment have the deep and rich love of a couple who has lived and loved faithfully for forty years. Deepened love depends on deepening acquaintance.

Such love, of course, faces hurdles. When we really learn to know each other, we discover faults and failures. We face disappointments. And it is love that enables us to move forward (or the lack of love that hinders us). Knowing, in other words, doesn't translate automatically into deepening love.

At the point of learning to know one another's faults, there are different ways of knowing. Discovering that the natives of Papua

New Guinea were perpetual, incorrigible thieves, missionary Otto Koning was frustrated and angry. Acquaintance did not make him more compassionate. After some years, through painful purging in his own heart, he came to see their thievery as linked to their spiritual bondage. In his selfishness he "knew them" as troublesome thieves. Aye, that they were. But when he laid down his rights, God gave him new eyes. Instead of protecting his possessions, he gave them away. Instead of constantly bickering with the natives, he was able to see them as bound by sin and needing God's love though him. It was the turning point in his mission work and led to the transformation and spiritual deliverance of many. And then he knew them even better—as brothers and sisters in Jesus.

When intimate knowing is joined to intimate love, we have a kind of knowing that is rich and validating. When intimate knowing is not joined with love, we have a knowing that we fear, a knowing that is laced with feelings of disappointment, shame, contempt, and hatred and leads to the awful experiences of rejection, manipulation, fighting, revenge, alienation, and betrayal. This is the risk we take in being known. It is why we fear and sometimes resist being known. It can feel safer to forever hide than to let ourselves be known.

With God, we have no option. He knows us inside out whether we are good or bad, whether we respond to Him or reject Him. He sees our shortcomings and is intimately acquainted with our failures—even before we stumble. He even arranges the events of our lives to search out and bring to light the deepest secrets of our hearts. But when we are His, His searching and knowing are joined to His loving. His knowing *about* is also an acquaintance *with* in a covenantal belonging. Even in our sin, even before our sin, He is working for our redemption because He is committed to our eternal good.

To be thus "known by God" in intimate, loving commitment is to be joined to Him in a bond stronger than marriage. Somewhere in this realization that God's all-knowing does not mean rejection but unwavering commitment, David breaks out in praise and worship:

> I will praise You, for I am fearfully and
> wonderfully made;
> Marvelous are Your works,

And that my soul knows very well.
My frame was not hidden from You,
    When I was made in secret,
    And skillfully wrought in the lowest parts of the earth.
Your eyes saw my substance, being yet unformed.
    And in Your book they all were written,
    The days fashioned for me,
    When as yet there were none of them.
How precious also are Your thoughts to me, O God!
    How great is the sum of them!
If I should count them, they would be more in number
        than the sand;
    When I awake, I am still with You.
        Psalm 139:14–18

To be known by God in the intimate sense is a treasure beyond all telling. It is to go to sleep with the realization that nothing can happen to us outside His watchful eye. It is to awake with the realization of eternal presence, Heaven's gaze fully upon us and Heaven's compassionate heart fully aware of our needs for the day. Think of the most faithful lover, the most caring companion, the best friend a man or woman could ever have, and the all-knowing God is more. He can be there when others need to leave. He can speak to us when words in the language of humans fall far short of what our hearts need. He remembers when others forget. God's all-knowing informs and enables His all-loving.

The end of the psalm returns to God's all-knowing, but instead of uncomfortableness or consternation or dread, David begs for the scrutiny:

Search me, O God, and know my heart;
    Try me, and know my anxieties;
And see if there is any wicked way in me,
    And lead me in the way everlasting.
        Psalm 139: 23, 24

God's acquaintance with our most secret desires, our hidden intentions, and even our sins does not diminish His love for us. He is committed to restoring His own. And David asks to be searched. It's the same word he used in the beginning of the psalm. Ransack me! Turn me inside out, upside down. Leave no door unopened. David understood that to be known by God is to encounter His covenantal commitment, to experience His limitless love!

But think with me for a moment. David's acquaintance with God's love was far short of what we know today. We now know God's commitment to us was so vast and deep He gave His Son, who lived among us, acquainted Himself with our sorrows, healed our sicknesses, took our stripes on His back, and poured out His life for us. He did this for us, not merely to forgive us, but to bring us back into the divine family!

And God didn't stop there. He poured out His Holy Spirit on those who received His Son by faith—the Spirit of life and peace, the Spirit of holiness, the Spirit of grace. This Holy Spirit of God living in us stamps us with the divine seal of ownership. We are His! He teaches us truth, speaks words of promise, offers divine guidance in dark places, empowers us to do what we cannot do, and leads us into the way of living like Jesus. This means we, like Jesus, give our lives and resources to lifting up those who are cast down, freeing the captives, advancing God's reign, forgiving those who hurt us, praying for those who despise us, blessing and doing good to those who curse us, and loving those around us.

If David could bless the all-knowing God and invite His searchlight under a covenant where animals died for his sins, what kind of humble, heartfelt prayers and praises ought to be erupting from our lips, knowing God's sacrificial love as we do today! Here's an attempt to update David's psalm with more recent data on what goes on in the womb and the eye-popping revelations of God in Jesus:

> I will praise you, O Lord, for You have designed me . . .
> The color of my hair
> The color of my eyes
> The shape of my nose
> My height

The build of my body
All my internal organs and glands that do their job
without me even thinking about them.

You programmed all this into my DNA,
into my chromosomes and genes
with their recessive traits and dominant traits.

I can't even see a cell—it is so small,
but You put together all this information and imprinted it on my cells
in strands and formulas so complicated that scientists
have spent decades studying them,
have employed computers to manage the complexity of the data,
and still can't figure it all out.

Such knowledge is too wonderful for me!

And besides the physical design of my body,
You put together my feelings, my moods, my ability to think
and reason and decide and dream and plan and choose
and laugh and cry and believe and hope.
You know my soul, my mind, my heart.
And You gave me a conscience, the ability to distinguish between right and wrong.
You made me spirit—more than physicality—
giving me the capacity to know You,
to interact with You, to hear Your voice, and to worship.

Such knowledge is way, way beyond me!

And then You saw my sin—
my helpless, hopeless condition,

the death sentence hanging over me—
mine, ours, millions in the dark.
And you sent Your Son to do search and rescue,
into hostile territory
with love His major weapon.
And we, the very ones He came to save,
rejected Him, scorned Him, put Him to shameful death.
And Your obedient Son went into death
and swallowed the powers of evil.

But He was Life and Resurrection,
and death was but a skeleton
crushed to dust,
its power and all surrounding powers
were broken in defeat.
And in the shining Light, Life was raised high for all.

In that glorious light of the glory of Your Son,
You called me to repentance.
You gave me the ability to believe
and imparted to me the grace to respond.
And upon my faith, You made my spirit alive,
opened my spiritual eyes,
unstopped my spiritual ears,
softened my hardened heart,
cleared my darkened mind.
And the first thing You said to me was, "You are mine!"
In that declaration was love . . .
and forgiveness and righteousness and holiness.
In that declaration was a pouring out of Your Holy Spirit,
entering my innermost being to take up residence in me,
transforming me, changing me instantly and continuously,

and every day telling me that I am Your child,
that You are my Father,
that I should call you "Papa."
YOU—who made the heavens and the earth!
YOU—who are so big the heavens cannot contain You!
You call me Your child,
You are my Father,
And You live inside of me.

Such knowledge is so far beyond me, I fall at Your feet
to worship You forever!

I truly am fearfully and wonderfully made . . . and
remade . . .
and I love my Maker!
Amen and amen!

Reflecting on the blessings of being known by God, Tozer says:

> And to us who have fled for refuge to lay hold upon the hope that is set before us in the gospel, how unutterably sweet is the knowledge that our Heavenly Father knows us completely. . . . Our Father in heaven knows our frame and remembers that we are dust. He knew our inborn treachery, and for His own sake engaged to save us (Isaiah 48:8–11). His only begotten Son, when He walked among us, felt our pains in their naked intensity of anguish. His knowledge of our afflictions and adversities is more than theoretical; it is personal, warm, and compassionate. Whatever else may befall us, God knows and cares as no one else can.[1]

Examples of God's omniscience

Through the Scriptures, we find many windows into God's omniscience. Here's a brief on-the-job overview of God's all-knowing.

1. God knows individuals—both the righteous and the unrighteous. Abraham: "For I have known [Abraham], in order that he may command his children and his household after him, that they keep the way of the Lord, to do righteousness and justice, that the Lord may bring to Abraham what He has spoken to him" (Genesis 18:19). God knew Abraham, even before the fulfillment of the promise, as the father of a great nation through whom God would reveal His righteousness and ultimately pour out Heaven's best on the world. (Note: Some modern translations render this passage in Genesis as God saying, "I have chosen him." Although the Hebrew word *yada* has broad usage, it is the same word David uses in Psalm 139—"known.")

Moses: When Moses was having such a round of it with the idol-making Israelites, persuading God both to spare them and to keep His presence with them, he also asked for deeper acquaintance with God: "that I may know You and that I may find grace in Your sight" (Exodus 33:13). Actually, it's the request one would make for audience with the highest of rulers: "that I may find grace in Your sight." What floods of relief and gratitude and unworthy joy must have coursed through Moses as God responded, "I will also do this thing that you have spoken; for you have found grace in My sight, and I know you by name" (v. 17).

Sennacherib, king of Assyria, spouted blasphemies against Israel's God and boasted that God's people didn't have a chance against his army. Through Isaiah, God declared, "I know your dwelling place, your going out and your coming in, and your rage against Me" (2 Kings 19:27). The big boasts Sennacherib made man-to-man were to God like the squeaking of a mouse against a lion it cannot see. God knew every move Sennacherib made, every thought passing through his proud head, and God's infinite knowing was exactly in sync with His infinite power. The swaggering braggart was toast and didn't know it.

Solomon: When David turned over the throne to his son Solomon, he assured and at the same time warned Solomon of God's omniscience. "As for you, my son Solomon, know the God of your father, and serve Him with a loyal heart and with a willing mind; for the Lord searches all hearts and understands all the intent of the thoughts.

If you seek Him, He will be found by you; but if you forsake Him, He will cast you off forever" (1 Chronicles 28:9). Unfortunately Solomon didn't keep that advice in mind in the years that followed.

Through Jeremiah, God foretold the terrible deaths of Zedekiah and Ahab, two false prophets among the exiles. These men claimed to be offering messages from God, even while using their position as prophets to have sex with other men's wives. "And because of them a curse shall be taken up by all the captivity of Judah who are in Babylon, saying, 'The Lord make you like Zedekiah and Ahab, whom the king of Babylon roasted in the fire'; because they have done disgraceful things in Israel, have committed adultery with their neighbors' wives, and have spoken lying words in My name, which I have not commanded them. Indeed I know, and am a witness, says the Lord" (Jeremiah 29:22, 23). God knew their lies, their secret motivations, and their outrageous sins. It is the height of stupidity to think we can actually have a private life and get away with it.

2. God not only knows individuals, but also He understands the needs, attitudes, and sins of people groups.

God assured Moses that He was fully acquainted with the miserable conditions of His people in Egypt. "I have surely seen the oppression of My people who are in Egypt, and have heard their cry because of their taskmasters, for I know their sorrows" (Exodus 3:7). What a comfort that God was intimately aware of the forced labor, the harsh demands, the cruel plots, the beatings, and the untold tears of the Israelites. But read on.

God also knew the weaknesses and sinful bent of the Israelites. When Moses was transferring the leadership to Joshua, God looked into the future with His omniscient eyes and lamented, "When I have brought them to the land flowing with milk and honey, of which I swore to their fathers, and they have eaten and filled themselves and grown fat, then they will turn to other gods and serve them; and they will provoke Me and break My covenant . . . for I know the inclination of their behavior today, even before I have brought them to the land of which I swore to give them" (Deuteronomy 31:20, 21).

In similar vein, God's Word through Hosea slices to the quick in exposing the sins of His people:

"Hear this, O priests!
    Take heed, O house of Israel!
Give ear, O house of the king!
    For yours is the judgment,
Because you have been a snare to Mizpah
    And a net spread on Tabor.
The revolters are deeply involved in slaughter,
    Though I rebuke them all.
I know Ephraim,
    And Israel is not hidden from Me;
For now, O Ephraim, you commit harlotry;
    Israel is defiled.

They do not direct their deeds
    Toward turning to their God,
For the spirit of harlotry is in their midst,
    And they do not know the LORD.
The pride of Israel testifies to his face;
    Therefore Israel and Ephraim stumble in their iniquity;
    Judah also stumbles with them."
        Hosea 5:1–5

God knew their sin. From their treacherous motivations to their violent and unfaithful actions, nothing was hidden from His penetrating view. But they did not know Him. This is the tragic irony of sin—a terrible ignorance of a terrifying understanding. God knew their every sin down to the secret chambers of their hearts; they had no understanding of Him.

Obadiah was God's messenger to the people of Edom, who saw themselves as impregnable, lofty, above all people groups around them. God declared,

The pride of your heart has deceived you,
    You who dwell in the clefts of the rock,
    Whose habitation is high;
You who say in your heart,
    "Who will bring me down to the ground?"
        Obadiah 3

Secure in their "impregnable" fortress, they were not outside the scrutiny of the all-knowing God. He knew their proud thoughts, their haughty attitudes, and their arrogant ways.

King Nebuchadnezzar put all the wise men of Babylon under threat of death if they would not tell his dream. In that high-tension scenario, Daniel and his friends turned to the Lord, and God revealed the dream to Daniel. Daniel's outburst of praise includes this telling description of God:

> He reveals deep and secret things;
> He knows what is in the darkness,
> And light dwells with Him.
> *Daniel 2:22*

As the dream was revealed and interpreted, we see that God knew not only Nebuchadnezzar, but also the present and future world empires of Babylon, Persia, Greece, and Rome.

3. God's omniscience stands as a warning against our attempts to hide.

Although our hearts are so twisted we even deceive ourselves, God searches the heart, examines the mind, and understands our innermost being with better vision than we have looking at a basket of goods in broad daylight. Through the prophet Jeremiah, God declared,

> "The heart is deceitful above all things,
> And desperately wicked;
> Who can know it?
> I, the Lord, search the heart,
> I test the mind,
> Even to give every man according to his ways,
> According to the fruit of his doings."
> *Jeremiah 17:9, 10*

Here we see the direct tie between wickedness and the ability to "know." The heart that is steeped in sin cannot see accurately, and the more sinful the heart, the more is its danger of being deceived. This also shows us why God sees so accurately, for He is perfectly sinless. There is not even the shadow of darkness in His heart, and consequently, there is no dimness in His vision.

The psalmist, even without scientific understanding of the astounding intricacies of the human ear and eye, shows the irony of trying to say things or do things unknown to the Maker of the ear and eye.

> He who planted the ear, shall He not hear?
> He who formed the eye, shall He not see?
> *Psalm 94:9*

The writer carries this forward in verse 11, declaring that God knows all our thoughts. The Hebrew word translated *thoughts* includes imaginations, plans, and inventions, especially those that to us seem cunningly devised.

> The Lord knows the thoughts of man,
> That they are futile.

The prophet Isaiah issues this stern warning:

> Woe to those who seek deep to hide their counsel far
> from the Lord,
> And their works are in the dark;
> They say, "Who sees us?" and, "Who knows us?"
> *Isaiah 29:15*

In the next verse, he exclaims, "Surely you have things turned around!" and then he asks incredulous questions.

> Shall the potter be esteemed as the clay;
> For shall the thing made say of him who made it,
> "He did not make me"?
> Or shall the thing formed say of him who formed it,
> "He has no understanding"?

Our all-knowing God is fully aware of the pride of nations, their aspirations to build empires and plots to throw others down, the prejudices of one group against another, arrogant feelings and attitudes, even the subconscious group motivations and schemas by which we live and interact with others. Nothing is hidden from His sight.

4. God's omniscience is a source of great comfort for His people. The assurances are given throughout the Scriptures, plentiful and specific. As you read the following verses, let your soul marinate in the truth of being known. First, a few from the psalms and the prophets:

> The Lord knows the way of the righteous.
> *Psalm 1:6*

> The Lord knows the days of the upright.
> *Psalm 37:18*

> He knows our frame,
> He remembers that we are dust.
> *Psalm 103:14*

> The Lord is good,
> A stronghold in the day of trouble;
> And He knows those who trust in Him.
> *Nahum 1:7*

Jesus speaks comfortingly of being known. "Your Father knows the things you have need of before you ask Him" (Matthew 6:8; see also v. 32 and Luke 12:30.) And to make the point even clearer, Jesus later says, "The very hairs of your head are all numbered. Do not fear therefore" (Matthew 10:30, 31).

Jesus also speaks of the deeper knowing—of His complete and intimate acquaintance with those who belong to Him. "I am the good shepherd; and I know My sheep, and am known by My own. As the Father knows Me, even so I know the Father; and I lay down

My life for the sheep" (John 10:14, 15). In this belonging kind of knowing, Jesus is committed to those who are His in a love that will not quit. Ever.

The Apostle Paul likewise links the knowing with loving relationship. "If anyone loves God, this one is known by Him" (1 Corinthians 8:3). And to Timothy, a young church leader, perhaps unsure of himself at times, Paul assured, "The Lord knows those who are His" (2 Timothy 2:19).

Near the end of Peter's life and ministry, while expressing concern about false prophets ravaging the church, he took courage from the wonderful truth that "the Lord knows how to deliver the godly out of temptations" (2 Peter 2:9). Yes, He surely does! He's been doing missions of deliverance for thousands of years.

The Apostle John addresses yet another wonder of God's omniscience. His whole letter seems focused on assuring believers, often using the expression "by this we know." In uncertain times, in difficult relationships, knowing our personal failures, we can wonder at times if we truly are children of God. John calls us to living in love and walking in the truth, and he says that this kind of life is itself assurance that we are "of the truth" (1 John 3:19). Even so, sometimes we don't *feel* saved. Worse, we at times hear inner accusations against our imperfections and failures. And to address this, John turns to the glorious truth of God's all-knowing. "If our heart condemns us, God is greater than our heart, and knows all things" (1 John 3:20). Oh, praise Him!

Given all these assurances, when we cannot sense God, when He allows things into our experience that hurt or confuse us, we must not assume that He does not know, or worse, that He does not care. God knows. He knows the tiniest details. And He knows so much more than we do. It is in the assurance of His omniscience—knowing everything about us—and in the greater assurance of His loving acquaintance—knowing us as His own—that we find rest when we do not understand. We do not need to see everything or know everything when we belong to the One who knows and understands us perfectly. J. I. Packer writes, "Living becomes an awesome business when you realize that you spend every moment of your life in the sight and company of an omniscient, omnipresent Creator."[2]

This God who knows us so thoroughly, intimately, and lovingly calls us to know Him. Without His revelation, we could not penetrate the unknowing. But God has chosen to reveal Himself. Through Jesus He has ripped wide the curtain and invited us—no, called us—to enter. Still it takes a seeking. In the flesh, dependent as we are on flimsy substance that we can touch and see, we easily miss Him, doubt Him, misread Him, and even deny Him.

We need to be men and women who seek and do not quit. God is! And as David learned, He is nearer than we think. C. S. Lewis put it this way: "We may ignore, but we can nowhere evade, the presence of God. The world is crowded with Him. He walks everywhere incognito. And the incognito is not always easy to penetrate. The real labor is to remember to attend. In fact to come awake. Still more to remain awake."[3]

Knowing God is the most important knowing. As God said through Jeremiah,

> Thus says the Lord:
> "Let not the wise man glory in his wisdom,
> Let not the mighty man glory in his might,
> Nor let the rich man glory in his riches;
> But let him who glories glory in this,
> That he understands and knows Me,
> That I am the Lord, exercising lovingkindness,
> judgment, and righteousness in the earth.
> For in these I delight," says the Lord.
> *Jeremiah 9:23, 24*

Jesus said, "This is eternal life, that they may know You, the only true God, and Jesus Christ whom You have sent" (John 17:3). Knowing God is a journey. We don't get there in one step. Or five. We typically start, as it were, on an exhilarating mountain. The view is breathtaking. But we hit valleys. Climbing can be rough. Later, looking back from higher vistas, we realize the initial "mountain" was but a hill, a very small knoll in the journey.

Knowing the One who is infinite takes more than a lifetime. There is more in the eternal beyond. As Paul said in a flash of insight, "God, who is rich in mercy, because of His great love with which He loved us, even when we were dead in trespasses, made us alive together with Christ (by grace you have been saved), and raised us up together, and made us sit together in the heavenly places in Christ Jesus, that in the ages to come He might show the exceeding riches of His grace in His kindness toward us in Christ Jesus" (Ephesians 2:4–7). Ages of acquaintance to come, folks! That's what we are in for.

"For now we see in a mirror, dimly, but then face to face. Now I know in part, but then I shall know just as I also am known" (1 Corinthians 13:12). It's enough to set our hearts racing!"

WALKING WITH GOD

1. Read Psalm 139 meditatively. David seems at first to be amazed, almost depressed with the realization of God's omniscience and omnipresence. But by the end of the psalm he begs God to search him and do whatever is necessary to turn him inside out. What do you think factored in on both kinds of responses? In what ways have you come to realize God's omniscience, and how has it affected you? Has there been any growth in your appreciation of His omniscience? And do you think it is good to have both an element of fear and an element of comfort in this reality of God, or do you think believers should live always in the comfort of divine omniscience?

2. Read 1 John 3:1–3 and 1 Corinthians 13:11–13. What are your reflections on the progression of our knowing and our being known?

3. What songs do you know that explore God's omniscience (or omnipresence or omnipotence)? Spend some time singing or listening to these songs and pay attention to your interaction with God as you sing. Here's a hymn Isaac Watts wrote three hundred years ago:

   Lord, Thou hast searched and seen me through:
   Thine eye commands, with piercing view,
   My rising and my resting hours,
   My heart and flesh with all their powers.

   My thoughts, before they are my own,
   Are to my God distinctly known;
   He knows the words I mean to speak,
   Ere from my opening lips they break.

Within Thy circling power I stand;
On every side I find Thy hand:
Awake, asleep, at home, abroad,
I am surrounded still with God.

O may these thoughts possess my breast,
Where'er I rove, where'er I rest;
Nor let my weaker passions dare
Consent to sin, for God is there.

4. Reflect on your relationship with God.
   a. What has been the most profound movement in your heart toward Him as you've explored who He is?
   b. What attributes of God are most attractive to you or move you most?
   c. What attributes of God do you find most puzzling?
   d. As you think about continuing to learn to know God, what are some goals you have?
   e. What are the avenues, activities, places, or people who help you most in your acquaintance with God?
   f. What avenues (nature walks, Scripture, prayer, fasting, meditation, discussion with other believers, music) do you find difficult or less meaningful in attempting to connect with God? Do you want to explore any of these more in the weeks or months ahead?
   g. When you think about your journey into God, what excites you most?
   h. In what specific ways do you think your life might make others hungry for God?

Notes

1. A. W. Tozer, *The Knowledge of the Holy* (New York: Harper & Row Publishers, 1961), 63-64.

2. J. I. Packer, *Knowing God* (Downers Grove, IL: InterVarsity Press, 1973), 76.

3. C. S. Lewis, *Letters to Malcolm: Chiefly on Prayer* (San Diego: Harvest, 1964), 75.